2001

A BOOK OF
GRACE-FILLED
DAYS

MARGARET SILF

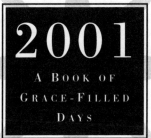

2001

A BOOK OF
GRACE-FILLED
DAYS

LOYOLAPRESS.
CHICAGO

LOYOLAPRESS.

3441 N. ASHLAND AVENUE
CHICAGO, ILLINOIS 60657

Published by Darton, Longman and Todd, London, UK, 2001
Copyright © 2001 Margaret Silf

Interior design by Kathy Kikkert

Library of Congress Cataloging-in-Publication Data

Silf, Margaret.
2001, a book of grace-filled days / Margaret Silf.
p. cm.
ISBN 0-8294-1490-8 (pbk.)
1. Devotional calendars. I. Title: Two thousand and one, a book of grace-filled days.
II. Title: Two thousand one, a book of grace-filled days. III. Title.

BV4812 .S55 2000
242'.2—dc21   00-035415
                                                                                                              CIP

Printed in Canada

01 02 03 04 05 / 10 9 8 7 6 5 4 3 2 1

INTRODUCTION

Jesus spoke of his words entering our hearts as seed falling to the ground. Some of these seeds are smothered by the distractions and preoccupations that grow over our hearts like weeds. Some fall on our hard patches, which are stony with resentment and unresolved conflicts. Some are carried away on the winds of our anxieties. Others, however, come to life and flower. These seeds take root in our hearts and experiences and continue to grow and come to fullness through our days, weeks, and years, transforming the very core of our being in the process.

Yet how easily these life-giving words can slip away and fail to germinate. When I find this happening to me, it helps to remember the Samaritan woman of the Gospel who met Jesus at the well (John 4:1–30). He was a complete stranger to her, yet he knew what was in her heart and he related her own story to her in a way that she had never heard it told before. She listened to his words, and those words became a

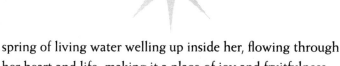

spring of living water welling up inside her, flowing through her heart and life, making it a place of joy and fruitfulness.

I believe that Jesus' words hold that same promise for us today, two thousand years after that encounter at the well in Samaria. They have the power to tell us our own story and to connect our life's experiences to the story of redemption. We are invited to listen to them and to reflect on what they might mean for us in the specific place, time, and circumstances in which we are living our lives today. Jacob's well is here and now, wherever we may happen to find ourselves. The encounter with the Lord is today and every day, continually taking us by surprise and calling us forward to take one more step beyond ourselves and toward God's kingdom. The living spring is ours to drink from and ours to share with a thirsty world.

2001: *A Book of Grace-Filled Days* is a little picnic basket to carry through the year. In this basket you will find a fragment of the living Word for every day, together with a short reflection that connects the words of Scripture to simple events, thoughts, or encounters in our daily lives. Together, the words of Scripture and the words of the reflection offer you a space to spend a few moments of your own with the Lord each day. Sit with him awhile at the well. Receive the seed of life that he offers in his words. Welcome the living spring that he opens up within your heart. Let him gently suggest connections between his Word and your lived experience. And then take the joy and the vision you have discovered back to your own family, town, or community, just as the Samaritan woman took the good news back to her people centuries ago.

If you are familiar with the lectionary readings used in the Anglican or Roman Catholic traditions, you will find that each daily text is taken from the lectionary readings for that day. The full references for these readings are provided on each page. Whether your tradition uses a set lectionary or not, 2001 is an opportunity to be in prayerful communion with other Christians, as together we read and reflect on the Word, which is God's gift to all of us. These fragments are small enough to carry with us through our busy lives, yet, because they are the Word of life, they are big enough to nourish our hungry hearts and to leave us with an overflow of love and grace to share with others.

I would like to thank all those who have in any way helped to put together this basket of fragments of Word and prayer, especially Morag Reeve, Helen Porter, and Hannah Ward of Darton, Longman and Todd, and all friends in North Staffordshire, for whom I originally wrote these daily reflections under the title *Potter's Clay*.

May you enjoy, day by day, the bread of God's Word, grown from the seed of his love for you. May it nourish you and open up for you the living spring that is yours alone to discover, yet which flows from the heart of God, where we all are one in him.

The LORD bless you and keep you!
The LORD let his face shine upon you, and be gracious to you!
The LORD look upon you kindly and give you peace!

— NUMBERS 6:24 – 26

A new year and another mile of the journey. Three hundred and sixty-five new chances to watch the sun rise on God's surprises along the way.

Numbers 6:22–27
Psalm 67
Galatians 4:4–7
Luke 2:16–21

Tuesday

JANUARY 2

• SAINTS BASIL THE GREAT AND GREGORY NAZIANZEN, BISHOPS AND
DOCTORS OF THE CHURCH •

*As for you, the anointing that you received from him
remains in you, so that you do not need anyone to teach you.
But his anointing teaches you about everything and
is true and not false; just as it taught you, remain in him.*

—1 JOHN 2:27

The touch of your truth on our hearts is the reason every
falsehood within us leaves us feeling exiled from our
real home in you.

1 John 2:22–28
Psalm 98
John 1:19–28

If you consider that he is righteous, you also know that
everyone who acts in righteousness is begotten by him.

—1 JOHN 2:29

Clarry was the most cantankerous resident in the
nursing home. Everyone kept out of her way.
But one day she caught me unawares and insisted
on showing me her album of photos of the
many stray cats she had once rescued and looked
after. It was Clarry who taught me that God
scatters his seeds even in the most neglected
weed beds and grows his greetings in the
most unlikely corners.

1 John 2:29–3:6
Psalm 98
John 1:29–34

The next day John was there again with two
of his disciples, and as he watched Jesus walk by,
he said, "Behold, the Lamb of God."

— JOHN 1:35 – 36

Let us be people who do not seek to hold our
friends' attention but rather to redirect
it toward you.

1 John 3:7–10
Psalm 98
John 1:35–42

Friday

JANUARY 5

• SAINT JOHN NEUMANN, BISHOP •

*Philip found Nathanael and told him, "We have found
the one about whom Moses wrote in the law, and also the
prophets, Jesus, son of Joseph, from Nazareth."
But Nathanael said to him, "Can anything good come
from Nazareth?" Philip said to him, "Come and see."*

— JOHN 1:45 – 46

We would never refuse to unwrap a gift because
we don't like the color of the wrapping paper.
Why, then, do we so often refuse to get to know
our neighbors, for no better reason?

1 John 3:11–21
Psalm 100
John 1:43–51

Saturday

JANUARY 6

• BLESSED ANDRÈ BESSETTE, RELIGIOUS •

And this is what he proclaimed: "One mightier than I is coming after me. I am not worthy to stoop and loosen the thongs of his sandals. I have baptized you with water; he will baptize you with the holy Spirit."

— MARK 1:7 – 8

We are the builders of a roadway, the cables along which the good news can pass. The One who follows is the One who leads, the Reality that makes sense of our pale shadows.

1 John 5:5–13
Psalm 72
Mark 1:7–11

[O]n entering the house they saw the child with Mary his mother. They prostrated themselves and did him homage. Then they opened their treasures and offered him gifts of gold, frankincense, and myrrh.

— MATTHEW 2:11

Carol paused for a moment and rested her hand on the head of her small son sleeping in the little bed. As she did so, she remembered the day. There had been a shaft of gold, when his laughter had broken through the grayness of her anxiety. There had been a moment of true prayer, when he had held his breath in delight as a robin hopped across the windowsill. There had been a time of pain and its healing, as she had soothed his grazed knee and kissed away his tears. Gold for joy, incense for prayer, myrrh for healing. Gifts from a child. Gifts for a Child.

Isaiah 60:1–6
Psalm 29
Ephesians 3:2–3, 5–6
Matthew 2:1–12

JANUARY 8

I, the LORD, have called you for the victory of justice,
I have grasped you by the hand;
I formed you, and set you
as a covenant of the people,
a light for the nations . . .

— ISAIAH 42:6

You place us here, where our lives are lived, as a pledge and a promise to those around us that you are with your people. Will our lives break that promise and snuff out its light, or will they keep it and bring it to fulfillment?

Isaiah 40:1–5, 9–11 or Isaiah 42:1–4, 6–7 or Acts 10:34–38 or Titus 2:11–14; 3:4–7
Psalm 29
Luke 3:15–16, 21–22

---

*All were amazed and asked one another, "What is this? A
new teaching with authority. He commands even the
unclean spirits and they obey him."*

— MARK 1:27

Sandra surprised everyone in her prayer group
by the power and authority with which
she spoke of her faith. She spoke your Word
with authority, because she knew you,
its author, as her own friend and guide.

Hebrews 2:5–12
Psalm 8
Mark 1:21–28

Rising very early before dawn, he left and went off to a deserted place, where he prayed. Simon and those who were with him pursued him and on finding him said, "Everyone is looking for you."

— MARK 1 : 35 – 37

David stopped for ten minutes in a quiet corner
of the parking garage before going into work,
just to let your peace settle in his heart and listen
to the murmur of your love. Punctually, at nine
o'clock, he went up to the office and into
an explosion of phone calls, messages, and
problems, but confident that ten minutes
in your silence would take him safely through
the demands of ten hours at his desk.

Hebrews 2:14–18
Psalm 105
Mark 1:29–39

JANUARY 11

*Encourage yourselves daily while it is still "today," so that
none of you may grow hardened by the deceit of sin.*

— HEBREWS 3:13

The kind word spoken into the moment of stress
tells me that you believe in me. It does
more than that: it reassures me that I can
believe in myself.

Hebrews 3:7–14
Psalm 95
Mark 1:40–45

They came bringing to him a paralytic carried by four men. Unable to get near Jesus because of the crowd, they opened up the roof above him. After they had broken through, they let down the mat on which the paralytic was lying.

— MARK 2:3 – 4

When I acknowledge my own helplessness and let you carry me, then new possibilities open up in the midst of impossibility, and healing can begin.

Hebrews 4:1–5, 11
Psalm 78
Mark 2:1–12

Saturday

JANUARY 13

• SAINT HILARY, BISHOP AND DOCTOR OF THE CHURCH •

*Indeed, the word of God is living and effective, sharper than
any two-edged sword, penetrating even between soul and
spirit, joints and marrow, and able to discern reflections
and thoughts of the heart.*

— HEBREWS 4:12

The two-edged blade of your Spirit slices
through my being, Lord, like the blade of a
master sculptor, ruthlessly stripping me of all
that hinders my growth in you, yet tenderly
revealing the shape and form of who I really am.

Hebrews 4:12–16
Psalm 19
Mark 2:13–17

*Now there were six stone water jars there for Jewish ceremonial
washings, each holding twenty to thirty gallons. Jesus told them, "Fill
the jars with water." So they filled them to the brim. Then he told them,
"Draw some out now and take it to the headwaiter." So they took it.
And when the headwaiter tasted the water that had become wine . . .*

— JOHN 2:6 – 9

We believe, because it is your promise, that you will
transform the water of our living and loving into the wine
of your Life and Love. But the miracle is only recognized
when we are poured out for others. If our wine stays in the
closed jars of our hearts, it might as well be water.

Isaiah 62:1–5
Psalm 96
1 Corinthians 12:4–11
John 2:1–11
Psalm 95

In the days when he was in the flesh, he offered prayers and supplications with loud cries and tears to the one who was able to save him from death, and he was heard because of his reverence. Son though he was, he learned obedience from what he suffered.

— HEBREWS 5:7–8

Sister Maria had faithfully recited the Divine Office through every day of her adult life. Then one morning she couldn't; her heart was too heavy and her spirits too low. She laid the book aside and let her desperate tears fall freely. They burned her eyes, even as they taught her a new depth of prayer.

Hebrews 5:1–10
Psalm 110
Mark 2:18–22

---

*[W]e who have taken refuge might be strongly encouraged
to hold fast to the hope that lies before us. This we have as
an anchor of the soul, sure and firm, which reaches into the
interior behind the veil, where Jesus has entered on our
behalf as forerunner.*

— HEBREWS 6:18 – 20

The slenderest thread of your life, surrendered
on Calvary, becomes a cable of love, strong
enough to draw us from death to life—the only
anchor that doesn't hold us fixed to the seabed
of our fallenness—the only anchor we can trust.

Hebrews 6:10–20
Psalm 111
Mark 2:23–28

[Jesus] said to the man, "Stretch out your hand."
He stretched it out and his hand was restored.

— MARK 3:5

The two young architects discussed their plans
as they made the train journey to the run-down
industrial town. Their skill and enthusiasm
was reaching out to restore withered dereliction
to new hope and community. I could see
your healing power flowing through their vision.

Hebrews 7:1–3, 15–17
Psalm 110
Mark 3:1–6

The main point of what has been said is this: we have such
a high priest, who has taken his seat at the right hand of
the throne of the Majesty in heaven, a minister of the
sanctuary and of the true tabernacle that the Lord,
not man, set up.

— HEBREWS 8:1 – 2

You dwell eternally with the Father, but the tent
of your living presence is also pitched in every
believing heart, so that God-with-us may travel
through an unbelieving world.

Hebrews 7:25 – 8:6
Psalm 40
Mark 3:7–12

I will put my laws in their minds
and I will write them upon their hearts.
I will be their God,
and they shall be my people.
And they shall not teach, each one his fellow citizen
and kinsman, saying, "Know the Lord,"
for all shall know me,
from least to greatest.
— HEBREWS 8:10 – 11

You write your truth in our hearts in a Word so
simple that a child may take hold of it,
yet so profound that it eludes our
highest understanding.

Hebrews 8:6–13
Psalm 85
Mark 3:13–19

For if the blood of goats and bulls and the sprinkling of a heifer's ashes can sanctify those who are defiled so that their flesh is cleansed, how much more will the blood of Christ, who through the eternal spirit offered himself unblemished to God, cleanse our consciences from dead works to worship the living God.

— HEBREWS 9:13 – 14

The glory of the summer roses had faded into a tangle of windswept autumn twigs. Jake cut back the dead wood and piled it onto the fire. This was not a time to regret the summer past, but to turn his attention to the needs of next springtime's growth.

Hebrews 9:2–3, 11–14
Psalm 47
Mark 3:20–21

Indeed, the parts of the body that seem to be weaker are all the more necessary.

—1 CORINTHIANS 12:22

You have protected our vital organs with the strength of our bones, our flesh, and our skin. Let us protect the apparently weaker members of our communities just as lovingly, and, in this way, allow their unique and vital truth, beauty, and meaning to be realized.

Nehemiah 8:2–4, 5–6, 8–10
Psalm 19
1 Corinthians 12:12–30 or 12:12–14, 27
Luke 1:1–4; 4:14–21

Just as it is appointed that human beings die once, and after this the judgment, so also Christ, offered once to take away the sins of many, will appear a second time, not to take away sin but to bring salvation to those who eagerly await him.

— HEBREWS 9:27–28

The story of our faith journey does not end in judgment, but in joy!

Hebrews 9:15, 24–28
Psalm 98
Mark 3:22–30

*But he [Jesus] said to them in reply, "Who are my mother
and [my] brothers?" And looking around at those seated in
the circle he said, "Here are my mother and my brothers.
[For] whoever does the will of God is my brother
and sister and mother."*

— MARK 3:33 – 35

In our kinship with each other, our loneliness
ends, but our responsibility begins.

Hebrews 10:1–10
Psalm 40
Mark 3:31–35

*Every priest stands daily at his ministry, offering
frequently those same sacrifices that can never take away
sins. But this one offered one sacrifice for sins, and took his
seat forever at the right hand of God.*

— HEBREWS 10:11–12

Claudia had been faithful in all her religious
observances since she was a child, but it seemed
to make no difference to her life. It was only
in the extremity of a crisis, when prayer was the
last thing on her mind, that a new kind of peace
broke through into her helplessness, taking
her heart by surprise and making the efforts of
her mind and will redundant.

Hebrews 10:11–18
Psalm 110
Mark 4:1–20

Praise the Lord, all you nations!
Give glory, all you peoples!
— PSALM 117:1

We carry the Light of the world in our hearts yet
often keep it confined to a single hour on
Sunday, when it so longs to spill out over every
moment of every day.

Acts 22:3–16 or Acts 9:1–22
Psalm 117
Mark 16:15–18

Those whose steps are guided by the LORD,
whose way God approves,
May stumble, but they will never fall,
for the LORD holds their hand.

— PSALM 37:23 – 24

The treasure at the center of our being needs no
defenses because it is indestructible. It is the
treasure that we only discover when we have
nothing left to lose.

2 Timothy 1:1–8 or Titus 1:1–5
Psalm 37
Mark 4:26–34

⋛ 26 ⋚

*All these died in faith. They did not receive what had been
promised but saw it and greeted it from afar and
acknowledged themselves to be strangers and
aliens on earth.*

— HEBREWS 11:13

Mother Teresa did not abolish poverty, nor did
Anne Frank set her people free. But their
journeys in trust, toward the distant star of
truth and love, carried the whole human
family with them.

Hebrews 11:1–2, 8–19
Luke 1:69–75
Mark 4:35–41

JANUARY 28

At present we see indistinctly, as in a mirror, but then face to face. At present I know partially;
then I shall know fully, as I am fully known. So faith, hope, love remain, these three;
but the greatest of these is love.

—1 CORINTHIANS 13:12 – 13

We can never truly see ourselves. The most we can see is our mirror image, and our mirrors, made by ourselves and for ourselves, are distorted by our own illusions. But when we see you, Lord, face to face, all intervening masks and mirrors will be removed. Then we will understand what it means to be loved perfectly in all our imperfection.

Jeremiah 1:4–5, 17–19
Psalm 71
1 Corinthians 12:31–13:13 or 13:4–13
Luke 4:21–30

He asked him, "What is your name?" He replied, "Legion is my name. There are many of us."

— MARK 5:9

Adam is known by many names. His children call him "Dad" and his pupils call him "Sir." His friends call him generous and his family call him extravagant. He calls himself angry and tender, and frightened and bold, confused and confident; he changes his names as often as he changes his mood. His true name, the name of his wholeness, is known only to you.

Hebrews 11:32–40
Psalm 31
Mark 5:1–20

JANUARY 30

*There was a woman afflicted with hemorrhages for twelve
years. She had suffered greatly at the hands of many
doctors and had spent all that she had. Yet she was not
helped but only grew worse. She had heard about Jesus and
came up behind him in the crowd and touched his cloak.
She said, "If I but touch his clothes, I shall be cured."
Immediately her flow of blood dried up. She felt in her body
that she was healed of her affliction.*

— MARK 5:25 – 29

When life has drained us to the point of helpless
desperation, your touch can heal. You heal us
by touching those hurting places that are
draining our energy.

Hebrews 12:1–4
Psalm 22
Mark 5:21–43

Jesus said to them, "A prophet is not without honor except in his native place and among his own kin and in his own house." So he was not able to perform any mighty deed there. . . . He was amazed at their lack of faith.

— MARK 6:4 – 6

Dare we invite the Lord to come into our church community today? Would he find, among us, his own, the faith that makes miracles possible?

Hebrews 12:4–7, 11–15
Psalm 103
Mark 6:1–6

*He summoned the Twelve and began to send them out two
by two and gave them authority over unclean spirits. He
instructed them to take nothing for the journey but a
walking stick—no food, no sack, no money in their belts.*

— MARK 6:7–8

We enter life, and we leave it, with nothing in
our hands, and we make our life's central journey
with just the staff of your love and your
grace to lean upon and to remind us that we
cannot take a single step without you.

Hebrews 12:18–19, 21–24
Psalm 48
Mark 6:7–13

Friday

FEBRUARY 2

"Now, Master, you may let your servant go in peace,
according to your word,
for my eyes have seen your salvation,
which you prepared in sight of all the peoples."

— LUKE 2:29 – 31

Every time we recognize the action of your love
in our world, the presence of your peace deepens
within us—the shalom of wholeness.

Malachi 3:1–4
Psalm 24
Hebrews 2:14–18
Luke 2:22–40 or 2:22–32

⇒ 33 ⇐

*The apostles gathered together with Jesus and reported all
they had done and taught. He said to them, "Come away
by yourselves to a deserted place and rest a while."*

— MARK 6:30 – 31

Our work and our ministries, that we find so
necessary and all-important, can lead us round
and round in ever-decreasing circles until
we come to that still point at the center, where
you say, "Stop! Rest with me a while."

Hebrews 13:15–17, 20–21
Psalm 23
Mark 6:30–34

Then I heard the voice of the Lord saying,
"Whom shall I send? Who will go for us?"
"Here I am," I said; "send me!"

— ISAIAH 6:8

Have you sent me, Lord? Or have I sent myself?
Did I arrive here because I listened to you or
because I thought I could arrange my life better
on my own? Am I carrying your message,
or am I transmitting my own?

Isaiah 6:1–8
Psalm 138
1 Corinthians 15:1–11 or 15:3–8, 11
Luke 5:1–11

FEBRUARY 5

• SAINT AGATHA, VIRGIN AND MARTYR •

*In the beginning, when God created the heavens and the
earth, the earth was a formless wasteland, and
darkness covered the abyss, while a mighty wind
swept over the waters.*

— GENESIS 1:1 – 2

George spent three-quarters of his life trying
to get himself in order before presenting himself
to you, his creator. Finally, frustrated by his
failure, he gave up his inner chaos to you in
despair, and then, at last, your Spirit could begin
its transforming action.

Genesis 1:1–19
Psalm 104
Mark 6:53–56

⊰ 36 ⊱

• SAINT PAUL MIKI, PRIEST AND MARTYR, AND HIS COMPANIONS, MARTYRS •

God looked at everything he had made,
and he found it very good.

— GENESIS 1:31

You declared that everything you had made
was good. What subtle pride, therefore, seduces
me into thinking that I alone am no good?

Genesis 1:20–2:4
Psalm 8
Mark 7:1–13

At the time when the LORD God made the earth and the heavens—while as yet there was no field shrub on earth and no grass of the field had sprouted, for the LORD God had sent no rain upon the earth and there was no man to till the soil, but a stream was welling up out of the earth and was watering all the surface of the ground.

— GENESIS 2:4 – 6

And before any of our life's shape is formed
or our circumstances determined, before ever
we can speak or think, your life wells up
in us, the origin of all we shall become in you,
and the first source of all that our lives
shall become for others.

Genesis 2:4–9, 15–17
Psalm 104
Mark 7:14–23

What your hands provide you will enjoy;
you will be happy and prosper.

— PSALM 128:2

What we make with the gifts you give us brings
us joy and leads to life.

Genesis 2:18–25
Psalm 128
Mark 7:24–30

⋑ 39 ⋐

The woman saw that the tree was good for food, pleasing to the eyes, and desirable for gaining wisdom. So she took some of its fruit and ate it.

— GENESIS 3:6

What we take that you have not given or seize that you have withheld brings us shame and leads to death.

Genesis 3:1–8
Psalm 32
Mark 7:31–37

They disappear like sleep at dawn;
they are like grass that dies.
It sprouts green in the morning;
by evening it is dry and withered.

— PSALM 90:5 – 6

Will the dream that is my life leave the
waking world the richer or the poorer for its
having been dreamed? Will the flower of
my years leave fragrance in its wake or will it
fade into forgetfulness?

Genesis 3:9–24
Psalm 90
Mark 8:1–10

Sunday

FEBRUARY 11

Blessed is the man who trusts in the LORD,
whose hope is the LORD.
He is like a tree planted beside the waters
that stretches out its roots to the stream:
It fears not the heat when it comes,
its leaves stay green;
In the year of drought it shows no distress,
but still bears fruit.

— JEREMIAH 17:7 – 8

What feels like an aching, unfulfilled desire is just the
growing pain of our own deepest roots, penetrating
the dark soil of our experience to find the water of their life
in you. The deeper the root darkness, the greener the
foliage and the more life-giving the fruit.

Jeremiah 17:5–8
Psalm 1
1 Corinthians 15:12, 16–20
Luke 6:17, 20–26

The LORD then said: "What have you done! Listen: your brother's blood cries out to me from the soil! Therefore you shall be banned from the soil that opened its mouth to receive your brother's blood from your hand. If you till the soil, it shall no longer give you its produce. You shall become a restless wanderer on the earth."

— GENESIS 4:10–12

What nation on earth is not soaked in
the blood of your brothers and sisters, Lord?
Their cries echo down the centuries, and
only the flow of your blood can bring healing
to our blighted hearts and homes.

Genesis 4:1–15, 25
Psalm 50
Mark 8:11–13

The voice of the LORD is over the waters;
the God of glory thunders,
the LORD, over the mighty waters.
The voice of the LORD is power;
the voice of the LORD is splendor.

— PSALM 29:3 – 4

When the cares and concerns of our lives engulf
us, Lord, and threaten to drown us in the tides of
despair, help us remember that your creating
Spirit, hovering over our chaos, is continually
bringing us to new birth and fresh growth.

Genesis 6:5–8; 7:1–5, 10
Psalm 29
Mark 8:14–21

"As long as the earth lasts,
seedtime and harvest,
cold and heat,
Summer and winter,
and day and night
shall not cease."

— GENESIS 8:22

Today may have felt like a disaster. This year
may have seemed like a failure. But our days and
years are held in a vast continuum of life,
and you have promised that this life is leading
all your children home to your eternal love.

Genesis 8:6–13, 20–22
Psalm 116
Mark 8:22–26

FEBRUARY 15

*God added: "This is the sign that I am giving for all ages
to come, of the covenant between me and you and every
living creature with you: I set my bow in the clouds to serve
as a sign of the covenant between me and the earth."*

— GENESIS 9:12–13

Give us the grace to see, beyond the stinging of
our tears, the radiance of your promise, eternally
shining through the clouds.

Genesis 9:1–13
Psalm 102
Mark 8:27–33

Friday

FEBRUARY 16

Then they said, "Come, let us build ourselves a city and a tower with its top in the sky, and so make a name for ourselves; otherwise we shall be scattered all over the earth." . . . That is why it was called Babel, because there the LORD confused the speech of all the world. It was from that place that he scattered them all over the earth.

— GENESIS 11:4, 9

Jim had plenty of time to look back over his life as he lived out his declining years in the nursing home, unvisited and unloved. In his heyday he had built a business empire out of nothing. He had made a name for himself. He had reached for the stars. But in the process he had lost all connection with his family and friends. They had scattered far and wide beyond his reach, and now he was a nameless old man, laid low by loneliness and regret.

Genesis 11:1–9
Psalm 33
Mark 8:34–9:1

Saturday

FEBRUARY 17

• SEVEN FOUNDERS OF THE ORDER OF SERVITES, RELIGIOUS •

Faith is the realization of what is hoped for and evidence of things not seen.

— HEBREWS 11:1

Carol was so proud of her son who had persevered through chronic illness and disability to become the wise and cheerful adult he had grown into. "I could only do it, Mom," he said, "because you believed in me."

Hebrews 11:1–7
Psalm 145
Mark 9:2–13

⋛ 48 ⋚

*"But to you who hear I say, love your enemies, do good to
those who hate you, bless those who curse you, pray for
those who mistreat you."*

— LUKE 6:27–28

"Lord, that I might love you," I prayed.

1 Samuel 26:2, 7–9, 12–13, 22–23
Psalm 103
1 Corinthians 15:45–49
Luke 6:27–38

⋙ 49 ⋘

Monday

FEBRUARY 19

• PRESIDENTS' DAY •

Then the boy's father cried out, "I do believe,
help my unbelief!"

— MARK 9:24

We may have beliefs enough to fill a catechism,
but do we trust you, Lord? We may believe in
everything we read on the seed packet, but will
we plant the seed? And will we tend its growth?

Sirach 1:1–10
Psalm 93
Mark 9:14–29

———————

⇒ 50 ⇐

"Whoever receives one child such as this in my name, receives me; and whoever receives me, receives not me but the One who sent me."

— MARK 9:37

The one who can see the bird inside the egg and the oak inside the acorn can see the Lord of all creation in a little child.

Sirach 2:1–11
Psalm 37
Mark 9:30–37

FEBRUARY 21

For whoever is not against us is for us.

— MARK 9:40

I would rather assume that everyone is friendly
and be fooled a few times but keep my
heart open to everyone around me, than hold
my prejudices and my wallet safe but die
with a closed-up heart.

Sirach 4:11–19
Psalm 119
Mark 9:38–40

Thursday

FEBRUARY 22

*"And so I say to you, you are Peter, and upon this rock I
will build my church."*

— MATTHEW 16:18

You build a community of faith upon the rock of
our hearts and lives, Lord. May that rock be a
steppingstone for all creation and never become
a stumbling block.

1 Peter 5:1–4
Psalm 23
Matthew 16:13–19

———————————

A faithful friend is a life-saving remedy,
such as he who fears God finds;
For he who fears God behaves accordingly,
and his friend will be like himself.

— SIRACH 6:16 – 17

James's parents were concerned about his friendship with
Gary. Gary was a troublemaker at school, and yet James
was always there alongside him, not in the troublemaking
but in the pain and punishment that followed after.
Only years later did they begin to realize how, gradually,
Gary had started to model himself on his faithful friend
and was slowly learning how to become a friend himself.

Sirach 6:5–17
Psalm 119
Mark 10:1–12

He forms men's tongues and eyes and ears,
and imparts to them an understanding heart.

— SIRACH 17:5

In the frantic circles of living there is a still
center that only our hearts know how to find.
Only in that still center will our thinking
become clear and true.

Sirach 17:1–15
Psalm 103
Mark 10:13–16

FEBRUARY 25

*It is good to give thanks to the LORD,
to sing praise to your name, Most High.*

— PSALM 92:2

As long as the earth spins, gentle hands will
wake the child from his sleep; strong arms
will lift the burden from a neighbor's shoulders;
warm words will soothe the friend in distress;
and a loving smile will fall like a blessing
upon the sleepless. Your hands, your arms, your
words, your smile, Lord, in ours.

Sirach 27:4–7
Psalm 92
1 Corinthians 15:54–58
Luke 6:39–45

Jesus, looking at him, loved him and said to him, "You are lacking in one thing. Go, sell what you have, and give to (the) poor and you will have treasure in heaven; then come, follow me."

— MARK 10:21

Arnold lay dying, surrounded by all his memories—everything he had valued and loved in life. Day by day he loosened himself from everything, saying good-bye with gratitude, not with regret. And when he was free of everything that held him, he was light enough to follow you into eternal life.

Sirach 17:19–27
Psalm 32
Mark 10:17–27

Tuesday
FEBRUARY 27

In works of charity one offers fine flour,
and when he gives alms he presents his sacrifice of praise.
— SIRACH 35:2

Marie received two gifts on Mother's Day. Her
older son sent her a bottle of expensive perfume,
gift-wrapped and dispatched by courier from
his company address in the city. Her younger
son, who still hadn't found a job, came round to
see her, gave her a hug, and said, "Thank you,
Mom. I love you."

Sirach 35:1–12
Psalm 50
Mark 10:28–31

Wednesday

FEBRUARY 28

• ASH WEDNESDAY •

Rend your hearts, not your garments,
and return to the LORD, your God.
For gracious and merciful is he,
slow to anger, rich in kindness,
and relenting in punishment.

— JOEL 2:13

Not a society for saints, but a meeting place for the broken. A community that acknowledges its needs and surrenders itself to healing. How many of us first came to God through a door marked "Accident and Emergency"? And how gently we were received, how lovingly tended. No recriminations, no interrogations. Simply God's overwhelming desire for us, that we might be whole again.

Joel 2:12–18
Psalm 51
2 Corinthians 5:20–6:2
Matthew 6:1–6, 16–18

I call heaven and earth today to witness against you:
I have set before you life and death, the blessing and
the curse. Choose life, then, that you and your
descendants may live.

— DEUTERONOMY 30:19

We may glimpse an astounding sunset sinking
behind the clouded horizon of a stress-filled day.
Right at the heart of shabby supermarket
consumerism, eager, generous hands drop their
contributions into the charity box. And a child's
trusting smile survives our grumblings. Little
pointers, showing the direction to Life.

Deuteronomy 30:15–20
Psalm 1
Luke 9:22–25

⋺ 60 ⋵

Friday

MARCH 2

This, rather, is the fasting that I wish:
releasing those bound unjustly,
untying the thongs of the yoke;
Setting free the oppressed,
breaking every yoke;
Sharing your bread with the hungry,
sheltering the oppressed and the homeless;
Clothing the naked when you see them,
and not turning your back on your own.

— ISAIAH 58 : 6 – 7

I may spend my life visiting the prisoners. I may write a
hundred letters to my congressman. I may study every book
on liberation theology. But if, my friend, I hold you captive
in my resentful memories, my heart remains a stone.

Isaiah 58:1–9
Psalm 51
Matthew 9:14–15

If you remove from your midst oppression,
false accusation and malicious speech;
If you bestow your bread on the hungry
and satisfy the afflicted;
Then light shall rise for you in the darkness,
and the gloom shall become for you like midday.

— ISAIAH 58:9 – 10

The grieving father of the victim of a terrorist
bombing murmurs, "I forgive them." A clenched
fist relaxes in shocked amazement and lets
the gun fall. And a strange new light flickers
through the darkened city.

Isaiah 58:9–14
Psalm 86
Luke 5:27–32

"The word is near you,
in your mouth and in your heart"
(that is, the word of faith that we preach).

— ROMANS 10:8

At the end of all our searching and at the
destination of all our journeying, we find you
waiting for us where we first began—in the
deepest stirrings of our own hearts. That is
where we hear you say, "The kingdom is very
near to you."

Deuteronomy 26:4–10
Psalm 91
Romans 10:8–13
Luke 4:1–13

Monday

MARCH 5

For I was hungry and you gave me no food.

— MATTHEW 25:42

We heard that you were hungry, and we called a
conference to discuss food vouchers. Father,
forgive! You looked lost in our neighborhood,
and we closed ranks. Father, forgive! You were
dirty and disheveled, and we complained
that our new shoes were hurting. Father, forgive!
There was a rumor that you might have
AIDS, and we took our child away from your
child's school. Father, forgive! We heard that
you were in prison, and we decided that it was
probably your own fault. Father, forgive!

Leviticus 19:1–2, 11–18
Psalm 19
Matthew 25:31–46

────────────

MARCH 6

The LORD is close to the brokenhearted,
saves those whose spirit is crushed.

— PSALM 34:18

The March winds play havoc with the newly sprung
daffodils. I bend to gather those that have been snapped
off in the night before their buds had a chance to open,
to bring them into the warmth and let them open
up their beauty. And a gentle voice whispers in the wind,
"If you care enough to do this for them, how much
more surely will I do the same for you?"

Isaiah 55:10–11
Psalm 34
Matthew 6:7–15

While still more people gathered in the crowd, he [Jesus]
said to them, "This generation is an evil generation;
it seeks a sign, but no sign will be given it,
except the sign of Jonah."

— LUKE 11:29

Jonah couldn't cope with your challenge, Lord.
And so he fled, right into the heart of the
storm. We know the storm and we know the
flights of panic. And we know how it feels
when the whale brings us back to the very same
beach from which we were running. Bring us
through the storms of faithlessness, back to the
beaches of surrender.

Jonah 3:1–10
Psalm 51
Luke 11:29–32

"Ask and it will be given to you;
seek and you will find;
knock and the door will be opened to you."

— MATTHEW 7:7

As the tree's branches grow in their desire to
reach for light and its roots grow in their delving
for water, so my heart grows in its desire for you,
its creator, and I find you in the process
of my seeking.

Esther C:12, 14–16, 23–25
Psalm 138
Matthew 7:7–12

My soul looks for the Lord
more than sentinels for daybreak.
— PSALM 130:6

The nights were long as my mother lay dying.
But then, at dawn, she would often fall
into a fitful sleep. I listened each night for the
first single birdcall before the dawn chorus
proper began, and I watched for the first flush of
sunrise over the garden. And then I would go out
for half an hour among the roses. I met you
there, among the roses, and you received all the
sorrows and the longings of the night into
your new-dawning love.

Ezekiel 18:21–28
Psalm 130
Matthew 5:20–26

───────────

*"You have heard that it was said, 'You shall love your
neighbor and hate your enemy.' But I say to you, love
your enemies, and pray for those who persecute you."*

— MATTHEW 5:43–44

As my friend walked away from me in anger,
I realized in grief that I had lost her love
because I had failed to heed your command to
let my love be all-inclusive. I had excluded from
my loving everything that caused me pain.

Deuteronomy 26:16–19
Psalm 119
Matthew 5:43–48

MARCH 11

[Jesus] took Peter, John, and James and went up the mountain to pray.
While he was praying his face changed in appearance and his clothing
became dazzling white.

— LUKE 9:28 – 29

I watched as a strong young man walked by, his arm
around the shoulder of an older man, stooped, frail in mind
and body, chattering meaninglessly, and ageless in
his suffering. I noticed a kind of clarity and openness in the
face of the younger man. He was walking slowly, matching
his pace to that of his companion. There was no sign
of impatience in his face or reluctance in his sheltering arm.
He was listening to the older man intently, as if to a guru.
I knew that Christ had crossed my path and that I had
seen his radiance in a city station.

Genesis 15:5–12, 17–18
Psalm 27
Philippians 3:17–4:1 or 3:20–4:1
Luke 9:28–36

Monday

MARCH 12

*Give and gifts will be given to you; a good measure, packed together,
shaken down, and overflowing, will be poured into your lap.*

— LUKE 6:38

Our containers are far too small for the fullness of grace.
We have two choices: either we turn aside from the
supply and settle for what we have, or we let it overflow
and flood the world around us.

Daniel 9:4–10
Psalm 79
Luke 6:36–38

*The greatest among you must be your servant. Whoever
exalts himself will be humbled;
but whoever humbles himself will be exalted.*

— MATTHEW 23:11–12

Who might merit the title today of this century's
greatest Christian? A picture comes to mind of a
small, gray-haired, vulnerable woman called
Teresa, going about her daily work in the dusty
streets of Calcutta. No status in the church.
No status in the world. No money, no family, no
power. Just an ordinary servant-saint.

Isaiah 1:10, 16–20
Psalm 50
Matthew 23:1–12

Wednesday

MARCH 14

"Can you drink the cup that I am going to drink?"

— MATTHEW 20:22

Sometimes we have to swallow very hard
when the bitter words or the hurtful comments
or the unjust accusations are flung at us.
And we remember a lonely man in a dark garden
who struggled with the bitter cup. "Share
my dying in the darkness," he calls to us, "and
you will share my resurrection at dawn."

Jeremiah 18:18–20
Psalm 31
Matthew 20:17–28

Blessed is the man who trusts in the LORD,
whose hope is the LORD.
He is like a tree planted beside the waters
that stretches out its roots to the stream:
It fears not the heat when it comes,
its leaves stay green;
In the year of drought it shows no distress,
but still bears fruit.

— JEREMIAH 17:7–8

With every prayer our roots reach deeper, searching for
the groundwater. With every act of kindness our branches
stretch a little farther to the sky, become a little
greener. Root and branch. Darkness and light. Praying
and living. Our wholeness and our fullness.

Jeremiah 17:5–10
Psalm 1
Luke 16:19–31

They said to one another: "Here comes that master dreamer!
Come on, let us kill him and throw him into one of the
cisterns here; we could say that a wild beast devoured him.
We shall then see what comes of his dreams."

— GENESIS 37:19 – 20

Dreams are like soap bubbles—so easy to
make, so easy to break. A child's dreams,
especially, are so vulnerable to the cold winds of
disapproval—from parents, teachers, and friends.
Walk beside us, Lord, and breathe your new
life into our broken dreams. Let your spirit turn
our deepest dreams into prayers.

Genesis 37:3–4, 12–13, 17–28
Psalm 105
Matthew 21:33–43, 45–46

While he was still a long way off, his father caught sight of him,
and was filled with compassion. He ran to his son, embraced him
and kissed him.

— LUKE 15:20

They found the runaway teenager in Singapore. After
a fight over a football match, he had taken himself halfway
across the world on his father's credit card. That's what
you could really call a family quarrel. Easy to imagine what
we might have to say to the lad if he were ours, when
he dared to come back—and perhaps not too difficult either
to imagine the surge of joy and the heartfelt welcome at the
airport when we received him safely home.

Micah 7:14–15, 18–20
Psalm 103
Luke 15:1–3, 11–32

*When the LORD saw him coming over to look at it more
closely, God called out to him from the bush, "Moses!
Moses!" He answered, "Here I am." God said, "Come no
nearer! Remove the sandals from your feet, for the place
where you stand is holy ground."*

— EXODUS 3:4 – 5

When heart speaks to heart, go barefoot and
respect the sacred space that lies open
and revealed between you. For you stand
on holy ground.

Exodus 3:1–8, 13–15
Psalm 103
1 Corinthians 10:1–6, 10–12
Luke 13:1–9

*Joseph her husband, since he was a righteous man, yet
unwilling to expose her to shame, decided to divorce her
quietly. Such was his intention when, behold, the angel of
the Lord appeared to him in a dream and said, "Joseph, son
of David, do not be afraid to take Mary your wife into
your home. For it is through the holy Spirit that this child
has been conceived in her."*

— MATTHEW 1:19 – 20

Whatever our plans may be, Lord, and however
well intentioned, keep our hearts always open to
the Dream that is known only to you.

2 Samuel 7:4–5, 12–14
Psalm 89
Romans 4:13, 16–18, 22
Matthew 1:16, 18–21, 24 or Luke 2:41–51

Tuesday

MARCH 20

*Then Peter approaching asked him, "Lord, if my brother
sins against me, how often must I forgive him? As many as
seven times?" Jesus answered, "I say to you, not seven times
but seventy-seven times."*

— MATTHEW 18:21–22

The difference between seven and seventy times
seven is the distance between time and eternity,
the bridge from conditional to unconditional
love, and the way from humanity to God.

Daniel 3:25, 34–43
Psalm 25
Matthew 18:21–35

⋛ 79 ⋚

Wednesday

MARCH 21

*"Do not think that I have come to abolish the law or the
prophets. I have come not to abolish but to fulfill."*

— MATTHEW 5:17

I expected you to throw away the old me
and start again from scratch to make me new.
But you are simply making me ever more
completely what I truly am.

Deuteronomy 4:1, 5–9
Psalm 147
Matthew 5:17–19

———————————

*This rather is what I commanded them: Listen to my voice
then I will be your God and you shall be my people.
Walk in all the ways that I command you, so that
you may prosper.*

— JEREMIAH 7:23

The crest of every hill revealed another higher,
more distant peak ahead, and there was
no end to the track marked out by the irregular
stone piles. We were frequently disheartened,
but we knew that the piles of rock pointed
the way—the only way—to the perfect view,
the vision, at the end of the journey.

Jeremiah 7:23–28
Psalm 95
Luke 11:14–23

Friday

MARCH 23

• SAINT TURIBIUS DE MOGROVEJO, BISHOP •

I will heal their defection,
I will love them freely;
for my wrath is turned away from them.
I will be like the dew of Israel.

— HOSEA 14:5 – 6

Dew is gentle. Dew falls silently, while we sleep,
softening our hard crusts so that grace might
penetrate our hearts.

Hosea 14:2–10
Psalm 81
Mark 12:28–34

"Let us know, let us strive to know the LORD;
as certain as the dawn is his coming,
and his judgment shines forth like the light of day!
He will come to us like the rain,
like spring rain that waters the earth."

— HOSEA 6:3

Ever so gradually the frozen earth thaws and the
furrows start to crumble. The March sun gleams
pale, clouds race, rain soaks and softens, and
our heart-seed wakes from its winter dreaming.

Hosea 6:1–6
Psalm 40
Luke 18:9–14

So whoever is in Christ is a new creation: the old things
have passed away;
behold, new things have come.

— 2 CORINTHIANS 5:17

Peter's hobby is woodturning. He can pick up a piece of rough timber from the wood yard and know with his fingertips the new thing that his skill can draw out of it. He has a vision of the grain and the color and the shape that only his heart's eyes can see as he clamps the block to the lathe. Would that he could realize that what he does for the wood, you, Lord, are doing for him.

Joshua 5:9, 10–12
Psalm 34
2 Corinthians 5:17–21
Luke 15:1–3, 11–32

---

*"Behold, I am the handmaid of the Lord. May it be done to me
according to your word."*

— LUKE 1:38

Our response to the call of your love is not made only for
ourselves but for all creation. It matters how we choose.
Our yes counts.

Isaiah 7:10–14; 8:10
Psalm 30
Hebrews 10:4–10
Luke 1:26–38

*Wherever the river flows, every sort of living creature that
can multiply shall live, and there shall be abundant fish,
for wherever this water comes the sea shall be made fresh.*

— EZEKIEL 47:9

When love begins to flow through the current
of our lives, the whole landscape of living starts
to change. There is springtime on our
riverbanks, and springtime leads to harvest.
We notice a new flower that we hadn't
seen before; we hear the meanings of silence and
read the unspoken signals in our friends' faces.
A tiny seed. A teeming harvest.

Ezekiel 47:1–9, 12
Psalm 46
John 5:1–16

Can a mother forget her infant,
be without tenderness for the child of her womb?
Even should she forget,
I will never forget you.
— ISAIAH 49:15

The wounded eyes of the abused child open
again, and trust flickers there momentarily.
There is a loving that is more powerful even
than all the hurting. Can this thing be?

Isaiah 49:8–15
Psalm 145
John 5:17–30

⋟ 87 ⋞

MARCH 29

How can you believe, when you accept praise from one another and do not seek the praise that comes from the only God?

— JOHN 5:44

When I was a child I lived under the constant need to please others. As I grew up, I more often chose to please myself. Only now do I begin to realize that all you ask of me is that I should let myself become what you created me to be.

Exodus 32:7–14
Psalm 106
John 5:31–47

*"Could the authorities have realized that he is the Messiah?
But we know where he is from. When the Messiah comes,
no one will know where he is from."*

— JOHN 7:26 – 27

The last thing we expected was to find you
sitting at the next desk, standing behind us in the
supermarket line, alongside us in the traffic
jam. We had our eyes fixed to the telescope, and
we failed to see the grass growing at our feet.

Wisdom 2:1, 12–22
Psalm 34
John 7:1–2, 10, 25–30

So the guards went to the chief priests and Pharisees, who
asked them, "Why did you not bring him?" The guards
answered, "Never before has anyone spoken like this one."

— JOHN 7:45 – 46

The author of all our being speaks with
authority. We recognize his voice at the center
of our reality. The center that cannot fail to
respond, whatever the cost.

Jeremiah 11:18–20
Psalm 7
John 7:40–53

Sunday

APRIL 1

• DAYLIGHT SAVINGS TIME BEGINS •

Then Jesus straightened up and said to her, "Woman, where are they?
Has no one condemned you?" She replied, "No one, sir." Then Jesus
said, "Neither do I condemn you. Go, (and) from now on
do not sin any more."

— JOHN 8:10 – 11

After you had sent them all away, we stood there
alone, face-to-face. My accusers had no more power over
me. Only one thing remained to obstruct the healing
flow of your forgiveness: my obstinate reluctance to forgive
myself and redirect my gaze away from me and toward
you, my healer.

Isaiah 43:16–21
Psalm 126
Philippians 3:8–14
John 8:1–11 or Ezra 37:12–14
Romans 8:8–11
John 11:1–45 or 11:3–7, 17, 20–27, 33–45

*"I am the light of the world. Whoever follows me will not
walk in darkness, but will have the light of life."*
— JOHN 8:12

When my heart is light, I go into my room
and light a candle; I close my eyes and I come to
you in prayer. When my heart is heavy, and
my hope goes dark, I struggle to manage without
you, until I stumble and fall and finally open
my eyes to find your hand upon me and a flicker
of candlelight reflected in your eyes.

Daniel 13:1–9, 15–17, 19–30, 33–62 or 13:41–62
Psalm 23
John 8:1–11 or 8:12–20

Tuesday

APRIL 3

"The LORD looked down from the holy heights,
viewed the earth from heaven,
To attend to the groaning of the prisoners,
to release those doomed to die."

— PSALM 102:19 – 20

You hang high above us, to reach us in our
depths. You are bound and nailed so that we
might become free. You are silenced into death
so that our cries might reach the Father.

Numbers 21:4–9
Psalm 102
John 8:21–30

"If you remain in my word, you will truly
be my disciples, and you will know the truth,
and the truth will set you free."

— JOHN 8:31–32

Your word falls as a seed into our hearts. Your
seed holds the secret of your deepest truth.
And your truth becomes the blossoming of our
eternal freedom.

Daniel 3:14–20, 91–92, 95
Daniel 3:52–56
John 8:31–42

Thursday
APRIL 5

• SAINT VINCENT FERRER, PRIEST •

I will render you exceedingly fertile;
I will make nations of you;
kings shall stem from you.

— GENESIS 17:6

When your Word takes root in our hearts, our
lives become an outgrowth of your truth,
releasing the seeds of your kingdom into the
waiting soil around us.

Genesis 17:3–9
Psalm 105
John 8:51–59

In my distress I called out: LORD!
I cried out to my God.
From his temple he heard my voice;
my cry to him reached his ears.

— PSALM 18:7

In our emptiest spaces God has the most room
to live and move and work his miracles.

Jeremiah 20:10–13
Psalm 18
John 10:31–42

≥ 96 ≤

"[I]t is better for you that one man should die instead of the people, so that the whole nation may not perish."

— JOHN 11:50

We made our own preparations for your entry to Jerusalem. We loaded our own guilt onto the back of the waiting scapegoat. It was the new girl, the quiet one, who got caught by the headmistress when we ran away. It was the colleague from the other department who was blamed for the mistakes we made. We believed it when they told us that the foreigners were taking our jobs and the homeless littering our streets. And then, when it was too late, there was blood on our hands.

Ezekiel 37:21–28
Jeremiah 31:10, 11–12, 13
John 11:45–57

Who, though he was in the form of God,
did not regard equality with God
something to be grasped.
Rather, he emptied himself,
taking the form of a slave,
coming in human likeness.

— PHILIPPIANS 2:6 – 7

Lord, change our grasping into giving, and our
desire for self-fulfillment into the courage
to be emptied so that there is space in our
hearts for you.

Luke 19:28–40
Isaiah 50:4–7
Psalm 22
Philippians 2:6–11
Luke 22:14–23:56 or 23:1–49

Monday
APRIL 9

Mary took a liter of costly perfumed oil made from genuine aromatic nard and anointed the feet of Jesus and dried them with her hair; the house was filled with the fragrance of the oil.

— JOHN 12:3

We pour out our grieving and rejoicing, mingled, over your feet. In a moment of intimate connection, we let your aching heart touch ours. A costly moment, for us and for you. A moment that releases a new fragrance of possibility.

Isaiah 42:1–7
Psalm 27
John 12:1–11

Peter said to him, "Master, why can't I follow you now? I will lay down my life for you." Jesus answered, "Will you lay down your life for me? Amen, amen, I say to you, the cock will not crow before you deny me three times."

— JOHN 13:37–38

You receive our eager gestures and intentions, knowing at once both the sincerity of our desires and the weakness of our wills. You know that our faithfulness will barely make it through the night. Yet you keep on loving us, beyond the cock's crow.

Isaiah 49:1–6
Psalm 71
John 13:21–33, 36–38

When it was evening, he reclined at table with the Twelve. And while they were eating, he said, "Amen, I say to you, one of you will betray me." Deeply distressed at this, they began to say to him one after another, "Surely it is not I, Lord?" He said in reply, "He who has dipped his hand into the dish with me is the one who will betray me. The Son of Man indeed goes, as it is written of him, but woe to that man by whom the Son of Man is betrayed. It would be better for that man if he had never been born." Then Judas, his betrayer, said in reply, "Surely it is not I, Rabbi?" He answered, "You have said so."

— MATTHEW 26:20 – 25

I dip my hand into your dish each week, Lord, and I come to your table faithfully, a believer in an unbelieving world. . . . Not I, Lord, . . . surely?

Isaiah 50:4–9
Psalm 69
Matthew 26:14–25

Peter said to him, "You will never wash my feet." Jesus answered him, "Unless I wash you, you will have no inheritance with me." Simon Peter said to him, "Master, then not only my feet, but my hands and head as well."

— JOHN 13:8–9

We cannot give to others what we have not been willing to receive ourselves. Give us the grace, Lord, to let you bathe us in your love, so that we may give that same love to each other.

CHRISM MASS:	LORD'S SUPPER:
Isaiah 61:1–3, 6, 8–9	Exodus 12:1–8, 11–14
Psalm 89	Psalm 116
Revelation 1:5–8	1 Corinthians 11:23–26
Luke 4:16–21	John 13:1–15

Friday

APRIL 13

*[O]ne soldier thrust his lance into his side, and
immediately blood and water flowed out.*

— JOHN 19:34

The stony Lenten path leads us to the point of
nothingness, where God himself is to be
destroyed. And in the moment of destruction,
the stream of Life is released, to flow forever
from the Son of Man to the people of God.

Isaiah 52:13–53:12
Psalm 31
Hebrews 4:14–16; 5:7–9
John 18:1–19:42

But at daybreak on the first day of the week they took the spices they had prepared and went to the tomb. They found the stone rolled away from the tomb; but when they entered, they did not find the body of the Lord Jesus.

— LUKE 24:1–3

A new day dawns and we set out into the unknown landscape of another day. The stones that blocked our vision yesterday are rolled away, but the Lord we seek is not in the prison of the past. He is walking ahead of us into everything the future holds.

Genesis 1:1–2:2 or 1:1, 26–31
Psalm 104 or Psalm 33
Genesis 22:1–18 or 22:1–2, 9–13, 15–18
Psalm 16
Exodus 14:15–15:1
Exodus 15:1–2, 3–4, 5–6, 17–18
Isaiah 54:5–14; 55:1–11
Psalm 30

Baruch 3:9–15, 32–4:4
Psalm 19
Ezekiel 36:16–28
Psalm 42; 43 or Isaiah 12:2–6, or Psalm 51
Romans 6:3–11
Psalm 118
Luke 24:1–12

So she ran and went to Simon Peter and to the other disciple whom Jesus loved, and told them, "They have taken the Lord from the tomb, and we don't know where they put him." So Peter and the other disciple went out and came to the tomb. They both ran, but the other disciple ran faster than Peter and arrived at the tomb first; he bent down and saw the burial cloths there, but did not go in. When Simon Peter arrived after him, he went into the tomb and saw the burial cloths there, and the cloth that had covered his head, not with the burial cloths but rolled up in a separate place. Then the other disciple also went in, the one who had arrived at the tomb first, and he saw and believed.

— JOHN 20:2 – 8

We search for you, but all we can find is the space in which we had tried to contain you. "You are looking for me in places of death," you tell us. "But I am the Life you can never contain within a fixed idea." Our world seems like a dark tomb too, Lord, and all we can find of you are the

wrappings and the trappings of how you might have been.
Yet we have seen! We have seen your resurrection
energy in a teenager paralyzed in a road accident, who
perseveres her way back to mobility. We have seen
your resurrection strength in the companion who stays
alongside us through our darkest hours and carries
the hope for us when our own resources fail. We have seen
your resurrection joy in a child's delight over the first
bluebells of spring. We have seen your resurrection hope in
the amazing ability of our earth to regenerate life year after
year in spite of our negligence. Lord, we see and we
believe! May we become, ourselves, the carriers of your
resurrection light into our world's darkness.

Acts 10:34, 37–43
Psalm 118
Colossians 3:1–4 or 1 Corinthians 5:6–8
John 20:1–9 or Luke 24:1–12 or, at an evening Mass, Luke 24:13–35

APRIL 16

*While they were going, some of the guard went into the city
and told the chief priests all that had happened. They
assembled with the elders and took counsel; then they gave
a large sum of money to the soldiers, telling them, "You are
to say, 'His disciples came by night and stole him while we
were asleep.'"*

MATTHEW 28:11 – 13

My lies may cost me dearly, but the truth will set
me free.

Acts 2:14, 22–32
Psalm 16
Matthew 28:8–15

Jesus said to her, "Mary!" She turned and said to him in Hebrew, "Rabbouni," which means Teacher.

— JOHN 20:16

Our teachers never told us this, Lord. Our books and courses never mentioned it. They taught us much about you. But we needed to hear you speak our name before we could know you and, in that knowledge, know ourselves. And when you spoke our name, our response was easy and inevitable, and uttered in our own familiar language.

Acts 2:36–41
Psalm 33
John 20:11–18

*And it happened that, while he was with them at table, he
took bread, said the blessing, broke it, and gave it to them.
With that their eyes were opened and they recognized him.*

— LUKE 24:30 – 31

Out of all the anguish and the turbulence of
our present moment and our present struggles,
a familiar gesture, instantly recognized,
slices through the confusion with a brilliant shaft
of light. Moments of clarity, restoring our
certainty that your presence, like the sun, is
always there, and only the clouds come and go.

Acts 3:1–10
Psalm 105
Luke 24:13–35

Thursday
APRIL 19

Then he said to them, "Why are you troubled? And why do questions arise in your hearts? Look at my hands and my feet, that it is I myself. Touch me and see, because a ghost does not have flesh and bones as you can see I have."

— LUKE 24:38 – 39

A ghost might have been easier to cope with—
more easily dismissed as a trick of the
imagination. But instead you ask for our real,
embodied, full-blooded response to your
indestructible Reality, which energizes every
particle of your creation.

Acts 3:11–26
Psalm 8
Luke 24:35–48

So Simon Peter went over and dragged the net ashore full of one hundred fifty-three large fish. . . . Jesus said to them, "Come, have breakfast." And none of the disciples dared to ask him, "Who are you?" because they realized it was the Lord.

— JOHN 21:11–12

There are still a hundred yards of water between me and the impossible invitation. My mind tells my heart to look before I leap, but my heart knows quite well who is cooking my breakfast.

Acts 4:1–12
Psalm 118
John 21:1–14

APRIL 21

*She [Mary of Magdala] went and told his companions
who were mourning and weeping.*

— MARK 16:10

What we have seen, we must tell. For there is
a world full of mourning, aching for the
touch of joy.

Acts 4:13–21
Psalm 118
Mark 16:9–15

And when he had said this, he breathed on them and said to them, "Receive the holy Spirit. Whose sins you forgive are forgiven them, and whose sins you retain are retained."

— JOHN 20:22–23

It was like climbing a rock face, trying to earn her forgiveness and her trust. And every time he reached the top, she pushed him off again, reminding him of how he had betrayed her. She held the keys of his heaven or his hell in her hands, and she chose to keep him captive in her unforgiveness.

Acts 5:12–16
Psalm 118
Revelation 1:9–13, 17–19
John 20:19–31

• SAINT GEORGE, MARTYR • SAINT ADALBERT, BISHOP AND MARTYR •

Jesus answered, "Amen, amen, I say to you, no one can enter the kingdom of God without being born of water and Spirit. What is born of flesh is flesh and what is born of spirit is spirit."

— JOHN 3:5 – 6

The seed of our immortal nature lies unfulfilled in the earth of our lives, until your Spirit awakens it to the promise of your eternal springtime.

Acts 4:23–31
Psalm 2
John 3:1–8

*"The wind blows where it wills, and you can hear the sound it makes,
but you do not know where it comes from or where it goes; so it is with
everyone who is born of the Spirit."*

— JOHN 3:8

I hear the rustling of my life's leaves and the creaking of
its branches. I feel the hardness of its fears and the warmth
of its loving. Yet everything that is me is brought to life
by the secret, silent, invisible sap of your Spirit, rising from
beyond me, raising me to beyond myself.

Acts 4:32–37
Psalm 93
John 3:7–15

He [Jesus] said to them, "Go into the whole world and
proclaim the gospel to every creature."

— MARK 16:15

You come to us in the intimacy of our everyday
living and then you send us out, like ripples
on the lake, to the furthest reaches of creation,
carrying the healing touch of your love
and your peace.

1 Peter 5:5–14
Psalm 89
Mark 16:15–20

When they had brought them in and made them stand before the
Sanhedrin, the high priest questioned them, "We gave you strict orders
(did we not?) to stop teaching in that name. Yet you have filled
Jerusalem with your teaching and want to bring this
man's blood upon us."

— ACTS 5:27–28

Those who ran away and hid, those who denied
you and abandoned you and crouched in the upper
room, afraid of the authorities, have been filled
with your risen presence, and all the world cannot
contain their courage and their joy.

Acts 5:27–33
Psalm 34
John 3:31–36

"So now I tell you, have nothing to do with these men, and let them go. For if this endeavor or this activity is of human origin, it will destroy itself. But if it comes from God, you will not be able to destroy them; you may even find yourselves fighting against God."

— ACTS 5:38 – 39

The enterprise they feared is ours today, and nothing can destroy it. Nothing can subvert the living God.

Acts 5:34–42
Psalm 27
John 6:1–15

*When it was evening, his disciples went down to the sea, embarked in a
boat, and went across the sea to Capernaum. It had already grown
dark, and Jesus had not yet come to them. The sea was stirred up
because a strong wind was blowing. When they had rowed about three
or four miles, they saw Jesus walking on the sea and coming near the
boat, and they began to be afraid. But he said to them, "It is I.
Do not be afraid."*

— JOHN 6:16 – 20

We have known the darkness of the lake and the fear
of the storm swell beneath our boat. Where are you, Lord,
when we row against the wind, and why, when you
come to our frightened hearts, do we so often fail to hear
your assurance: "It is I. Do not be afraid"?

Acts 6:1–7
Psalm 33
John 6:16–21

Sunday

APRIL 29

When it was already dawn, Jesus was standing on the shore; but the disciples did not realize that it was Jesus. Jesus said to them, "Children, have you caught anything to eat?" They answered him, "No." So he said to them, "Cast the net over the right side of the boat and you will find something." So they cast it, and were not able to pull it in because of the number of fish.

— JOHN 21:4 – 6

My nets seem to be empty most of the time. Perhaps it's because I think I know so much better than you how to manage my life and because I am reluctant to believe in the possibility of a miracle to starboard.

Acts 5:27–32, 40–41
Psalm 30
Revelation 5:11–14
John 21:1–19 or 21:1–14

So they said to him, "What can we do to accomplish the works of God?" Jesus answered and said to them, "This is the work of God, that you believe in the one he sent."

— JOHN 6:28 – 29

How much energy we expend in working out
what to do for you and how to do it! If we would
only rest in our believing and trust you to
open up each new step before us, how much
more fruitful our lives might be.

Acts 6:8–15
Psalm 119
John 6:22–29

Tuesday

MAY 1

• SAINT JOSEPH THE WORKER •

"I am the bread of life; whoever comes to me will never hunger, and whoever believes in me will never thirst."

— JOHN 6:35

For years I tried to live on the surface satisfactions and the candies of existence. Until I became painfully aware of the aching hunger at the center of my being. And gratefully, needfully, I stretched out my hands for the life-giving bread that alone could fill me and that you never cease to offer.

Acts 7:51–8:1
Psalm 31
John 6:30–35

*Saul, meanwhile, was trying to destroy the church;
entering house after house and dragging out men and
women, he handed them over for imprisonment.*

— ACTS 8:3

Nothing we can do, not the full sum of the worst
that we can perpetrate, can place us beyond
the ranging beam of grace.

Acts 8:1–8
Psalm 66
John 6:35–40

Philip said to him, "Master, show us the Father, and that will be enough for us." Jesus said to him, "Have I been with you for so long a time and you still do not know me, Philip? Whoever has seen me has seen the Father."

— JOHN 14:8 – 9

When I hold an acorn in my hand, I hold the encoded reality of the full-grown oak. So you too, Lord, carry the fullness of the Father in your human life, and you call us, your brothers and sisters, to carry his fullness in our lives.

1 Corinthians 15:1–8
Psalm 19
John 14:6–14

On his journey, as he was nearing Damascus, a light from the sky suddenly flashed around him. He fell to the ground and heard a voice saying to him, "Saul, Saul, why are you persecuting me?" He said, "Who are you, sir?" The reply came, "I am Jesus, whom you are persecuting. Now get up and go into the city and you will be told what you must do."

— ACTS 9:3 – 6

When your light pierces our darkness, it reveals not your condemnation, but first your questioning, then your challenge, and finally your guidance and empowerment.

Acts 9:1–20
Psalm 117
John 6:52–59

Then many of his disciples who were listening said, "This saying is hard; who can accept it?" . . . Jesus then said to the Twelve, "Do you also want to leave?" Simon Peter answered him, "Master, to whom shall we go? You have the words of eternal life. We have come to believe and are convinced that you are the Holy One of God."

— JOHN 6:60, 67–69

Our faith sometimes leads us into impossible corners and down impassable tracks. It seems like the end of the road. A Calvary moment. You ask us gently, "Are you going to turn aside?" And your very gentleness renews our inner certainty that yours is the only Way through the impossible.

Acts 9:31–42
Psalm 116
John 6:60–69

Sunday
MAY 6

My sheep hear my voice;
I know them, and they follow me.
— JOHN 10:27

Sometimes I know I am traveling in the
right direction, however foggy the day. Those
are the times when the compass of my journey
aligns exactly with the true north that is
planted in my soul; and when the echo of my life
unmistakably recognizes the voice that first
spoke it into existence.

Acts 13:14, 43–52
Psalm 100
Revelation 7:9, 14–17
John 10:27–30

*"I came so that they might have life and have it
more abundantly."*

— JOHN 10:10

Dare we entrust ourselves to the empty spaces
we must cross, to discover the fullness that is
waiting for us, even now, right where we are?

Acts 11:1–18
Psalm 42
John 10:1–10

*So the Jews gathered around him and said to him, "How
long are you going to keep us in suspense? If you are the
Messiah, tell us plainly." Jesus answered them, "I told you
and you do not believe."*

— JOHN 10:24 – 25

A clear, unambiguous sign from God would
change the world, like a universal change
of government. But the Christ brings us
something more permanent and more true:
a change of heart.

Acts 11:19–26
Psalm 87
John 10:22–30

Wednesday

MAY 9

*Jesus cried out and said, "Whoever believes in me believes
not only in me but also in the one who sent me, and
whoever sees me sees the one who sent me."*

— JOHN 12:44 – 45

I read the letter from my friend over and over
again. It bridged the miles between us. A word
from her, and I felt we were once more
sharing our life's journey. How much more surely
does your Word, incarnate in your Son, bring
me into your living presence?

Acts 12:24–13:5
Psalm 67
John 12:44–50

─────────────

*"Amen, amen, I say to you, whoever receives the one I send
receives me, and whoever receives me receives the
one who sent me."*

— JOHN 13:20

The lone parent was new to the district. After
the service was over, she left the church
alone, with her boisterous toddler. The regular
congregation wondered who she was, but
nobody took the trouble to find out.
Strange, that you should be unwelcome in
your own house.

Acts 13:13–25
Psalm 89
John 13:16–20

Thomas said to him, "Master, we do not know where you are going; how can we know the way?" Jesus said to him, "I am the way and the truth and the life. No one comes to the Father except through me."

— JOHN 14:5 – 6

I don't need to know the way; I am on a journey where everyone I meet is my destination, for in everyone I meet, I meet you.

Acts 13:26–33
Psalm 2
John 14:1–6

• SAINTS NEREUS AND ACHILLEUS, MARTYRS • SAINT PANCRAS, MARTYR •

*"Do you not believe that I am in the Father and
the Father is in me? The words that I speak to you I do not
speak on my own. The Father who dwells in me is doing
his works."*

— JOHN 14:10

It is an inner voice as familiar as our own.
Listen to this voice and let it work in the world
through you.

Acts 13:44–52
Psalm 98
John 14:7–14

⋟ 133 ⋞

*"I give you a new commandment: love one another. As I
have loved you, so you also should love one another. This
is how all will know that you are my disciples, if you have
love for one another."*

— JOHN 13:34 – 35

He doesn't ask us to counsel or instruct each
other, to guide or to direct or solve each other's
problems. He asks us only to receive each
other with the open arms of love, and leave the
rest to him.

Acts 14:21–27
Psalm 145
Revelation 21:1–5
John 13:31–35

Monday

MAY 14

• SAINT MATTHIAS, APOSTLE •

It was not you who chose me, but I who chose you and
appointed you to go and bear fruit that will remain, so that
whatever you ask the Father in my name he may give you.
This I command you: love one another.

— JOHN 15:16 – 17

Everything comes from you, Lord. You choose.
You send us out. You make us fruitful. All you ask
of us is that we respond to all with love.

Acts 1:15–17, 20–26
Psalm 113
John 15:9–17

Tuesday

MAY 15

Peace I leave with you; my peace I give to you. Not as the
world gives do I give it to you. Do not let your hearts be
troubled or afraid.

— JOHN 14:27

When we live in your peace, the conflicts of our
lives—both inside and outside ourselves—
don't go away. Instead you draw us into
the still center at the heart of the storm, where
healing can begin.

Acts 14:19–28
Psalm 145
John 14:27–31

*I am the vine, you are the branches. Whoever remains in
me and I in him will bear much fruit, because without me
you can do nothing.*

— JOHN 15:5

The forest is carpeted with bluebells. Every May
they flood my heart with their joyful exuberance
of blue. Year in, year out, their fragile bulbs
break out again into the fullness of their living.
Yet how dispiriting is the sight of a jug of
bluebells, plucked at dawn, and by midday,
drooping sadly down to premature death.

Acts 15:1–6
Psalm 122
John 15:1–8

"As the Father loves me, so I also love you. Remain in my love. If you keep my commandments, you will remain in my love, just as I have kept my Father's commandments and remain in his love. I have told you this so that my joy may be in you and your joy may be complete."

— JOHN 15:9 – 11

To keep your commandments is to obey the deepest dictates of my heart, as a stream obeys its deepest impulse when it courses down toward the ocean, watering the land as it flows.

Acts 15:7–21
Psalm 96
John 15:9–11

Friday
MAY 18

• SAINT JOHN I, POPE AND MARTYR •

It was not you who chose me, but I who chose you and
appointed you to go and bear fruit that will remain, so that
whatever you ask the Father in my name he may give you.

— JOHN 15:16

The mother watched patiently as her child
made his options. Choosing subjects, choosing
a job, choosing friends. He was sure that
he was in control, yet she had made the choice
that made all other choices possible: the
choice to give him life.

Acts 15:22–31
Psalm 57
John 15:12–17

"Remember the word I spoke to you, 'No slave is greater than his master.' If they persecuted me, they will also persecute you. If they kept my word, they will also keep yours."

— JOHN 15:20

When we run up against the rock face, let us remember that you ran up against it too. You were broken against it so that the seeds of eternal life might be released. Seeds that settle and take root in the rocks of persecution, breaking down the hardness, bringing life.

Acts 16:1–10
Psalm 100
John 15:18–21

The Advocate, the holy Spirit that the Father will send in my name—he will teach you everything and remind you of all that (I) told you.

— JOHN 14:26

When you shed your light back over the landmarks of our journeys, reminding us of those sacred moments when we have been touched by your love, then we know that we are feeling the breath of your Spirit.

Acts 15:1–2, 22–29
Psalm 67
Revelation 21:10–14, 22–23
John 14:23–29

"When the Advocate comes whom I will send you from the Father, the Spirit of truth that proceeds from the Father, he will testify to me. And you also testify, because you have been with me from the beginning."

— JOHN 15:26 – 27

The Spirit is your witness, giving us evidence, in our own lived experience, of your Reality. Shall our lives, too, provide such living evidence to others?

Acts 16:11–15
Psalm 149
John 15:26–16:4

*"But now I am going to the one who sent me, and not one
of you asks me, 'Where are you going?' But because I told
you this, grief has filled your hearts. But I tell you the
truth, it is better for you that I go. For if I do not go,
the Advocate will not come to you. But if I go,
I will send him to you."*

— JOHN 16:5 – 7

In the dark times of our prayer you seem to
have withdrawn far beyond the reach of
our minds and senses. Yet the darkness reveals
the stars, and the cloud that receives you
holds the promise of an unimaginable new
dawning of power and love.

Acts 16:22–34
Psalm 138
John 16:5–11

"[H]e is not far from any one of us. For 'In him we live
and move and have our being.'"

— ACTS 17:27–28

The tiny oak leaves are just beginning to unfurl,
waking up to springtime. If I could tell them
about the vast network of branch and trunk and
root that holds them in being, they would never
believe me. An obvious reality for me—an
impossible leap of imagination for them. How
far am I, then, from understanding the sources of
your love that hold me in being?

Acts 17:15, 22–18:1
Psalm 148
John 16:12–15

Then he led them (out) as far as Bethany, raised his hands,
and blessed them. As he blessed them he parted from them
and was taken up to heaven. They did him homage and
then returned to Jerusalem with great joy.

— LUKE 24:50 – 52

As the train was about to depart, he held her
close and assured her of his love. As it drew
away from the station, he waved his blessing
upon her. Her heart was aching, but she
cherished the parting embrace deep in her heart.
It planted joy into the heartache and trust into
the promise of his return.

Acts 1:1–11
Psalm 47
Ephesians 1:17–23 or Ephesians 4:1–13 or 4:1–7, 11–13
Luke 24:46–53

MAY 25

When a woman is in labor, she is in anguish because her hour has arrived; but when she has given birth to a child, she no longer remembers the pain because of her joy that a child has been born into the world. So you also are now in anguish. But I will see you again, and your hearts will rejoice, and no one will take your joy away from you.

— JOHN 16:21 – 22

The final stage of labor seemed to last for hours. I started to think, "This child isn't ever going to be born," but my common sense knew better. When I start to wonder whether your kingdom will ever come, I remember the moment when the midwife placed my daughter in my arms. And I believe.

Acts 18:9–18
Psalm 47
John 16:20–23

Saturday

MAY 26

• SAINT PHILIP NERI, PRIEST •

*[A]sk and you will receive, so that your joy
may be complete.*

— JOHN 16:24

I asked for food and you taught me how
to fish. I asked for security and you gave me the
freedom to live without fear. I asked for
happiness and you gave me joy. I come to you
with the leaves and petals of my desires, but
you satisfy their roots.

Acts 18:23–28
Psalm 47
John 16:23–28

Sunday

MAY 27

Let the one who thirsts come forward, and the one who
wants it receive the gift of life-giving water.

— REVELATION 22:17

Water, source of life, without droughts
or water towers, without bills, and without
shareholders. The only qualification for
receiving it is to want it.

Acts 7:55–60
Psalm 97
Revelation 22:12–14, 16–17, 20
John 17:20–26

Monday

MAY 28

• MEMORIAL DAY •

*"I have told you this so that you might have peace in me.
In the world you will have trouble, but take courage, I
have conquered the world."*

— JOHN 16:33

The more comfortable we feel in our
believing and the practice of our faith, the more
likely we are to be drifting away from you.
Give us rather the peace that takes us past the
comfort, through disturbance, into courage,
toward the truth.

Acts 19:1–8
Psalm 68
John 16:29–33

There you poured abundant rains, God,
graciously given to the poor in their need.

— PSALM 68:11

Not just watering cans to keep us going through
the hard times, but generous, soaking, saturating
grace that brings life out of our most deeply
buried roots.

Acts 20:17–27
Psalm 68
John 17:1–11

I do not ask that you take them out of the world but that you keep them from the evil one. They do not belong to the world any more than I belong to the world. Consecrate them in the truth. Your word is truth. As you sent me into the world, so I sent them into the world. And I consecrate myself for them, so that they also may be consecrated in truth.

— JOHN 17:15 – 19

Consecration . . . not a life taken out of the world, but a life commissioned to enter far more deeply into the world, carrying your truth and your love. Consecration . . . a call and a commission for every believer.

Acts 20:28–38
Psalm 68
John 17:11–19

*When Elizabeth heard Mary's greeting, the infant leaped in
her womb, and Elizabeth, filled with the holy Spirit, cried
out in a loud voice and said, "Most blessed are you among
women, and blessed is the fruit of your womb."*

— LUKE 1:41 – 42

When heart speaks to heart, the still-unborn
Christ in me leaps in recognition of the
still-unborn Christ in you.

Zephaniah 3:14–18 or Romans 12:9–16
Isaiah 12:2–6
Luke 1:39–56

"Amen, amen, I say to you, when you were younger, you used to dress yourself and go where you wanted; but when you grow old, you will stretch out your hands, and someone else will dress you and lead you where you do not want to go."

— JOHN 21:18

When I began my journey of faith, I felt strong and sure and I thought I knew where I was going. But the further I traveled, the more I became aware of my ever-growing helplessness and inadequacy, and my absolute need of you.

Acts 25:13–21
Psalm 103
John 21:15–19

There are also many other things that Jesus did, but if these were to be described individually, I do not think the whole world would contain the books that would be written.

— JOHN 21:25

And if each of us were to tell of all the ways the
Lord has touched our lives and our hearts,
the world itself could not contain all our stories.

Acts 28:16–20, 30–31
Psalm 11
John 21:20–25

Sunday

JUNE 3

• PENTECOST SUNDAY •

Then there appeared to them tongues as of fire, which parted and came to rest on each one of them.
And they were all filled with the holy Spirit and began to speak in different tongues, as the Spirit enabled them to proclaim.

— ACTS 2:3 – 4

The flame of your Spirit is divided to dwell in each believing heart, but in its division it is not diminished but multiplied so that the whole of your creation might catch your light and your fire.

VIGIL:
Genesis 11:1–9 or Exodus 19:3–8, 16–20 or Ezekiel 37:1–14 or Joel 3:1–5
Psalm 104
Romans 8:22–27
John 7:37–39

DAY:
Acts 2:1–11
Psalm 104
1 Corinthians 12:3–7, 12–13 or Romans 8:8–17
John 20:19–23 or John 14:15–16, 23–26

"But those tenants said to one another, 'This is the heir.
Come, let us kill him, and the inheritance will be ours.'
So they seized him and killed him, and threw him
out of the vineyard."

— MARK 12:7–8

What we take by force we may hold for a
season. What you give through grace is our
inheritance for all eternity.

Tobit 1:1, 3; 2:1–8
Psalm 112
Mark 12:1–12

Knowing their hypocrisy he said to them, "Why are you testing me? Bring me a denarius to look at." They brought one to him and he said to them, "Whose image and inscription is this?" They replied to him, "Caesar's." So Jesus said to them, "Repay to Caesar what belongs to Caesar and to God what belongs to God."

— MARK 12:15–17

How shall I draw my life's energy? In the currency of Caesar, with its punitive interest rates? Or in the currency of God, that is given unearned?

Tobit 2:9–14
Psalm 112
Mark 12:13–17

Make known to me your ways, LORD;
teach me your paths.
Guide me in your truth and teach me,
for you are God my savior.

— PSALM 25:4 – 5

The unique pathways that you walk with each of us are not on any map. Instead we must trust the compass you have planted in our hearts.

Tobit 3:1–11, 16–17
Psalm 25
Mark 12:18–27

JUNE 7

One of the scribes, when he came forward and heard them disputing and saw how well he had answered them, asked him, "Which is the first of all the commandments?" Jesus replied, "The first is this: 'Hear, O Israel! The Lord our God is Lord alone! You shall love the Lord your God with all your heart, with all your soul, with all your mind, and with all your strength.' The second is this: 'You shall love your neighbor as yourself.' There is no other commandment greater than these."

— MARK 12:28 – 31

All of me: not just the Sunday slot. All of me: not just my conscious thoughts. All of me: not just the span of years I call my life on earth. All of me: just space enough to hold a seed of God.

Tobit 6:10–11; 7:1, 9–17; 8:4–9
Psalm 128
Mark 12:28–34

Friday

JUNE 8

The LORD sets prisoners free;
the LORD gives sight to the blind.
The LORD raises up those who are bowed down.

— PSALM 146:7, 8

When we look into the eyes of one who is
caring for the oppressed, the hungry, the
prisoners, we are looking into the heart of God,
whether the one who is caring is aware
of God or not.

Tobit 11:5–17
Psalm 146
Mark 12:35–37

He sat down opposite the treasury and observed how the crowd put money into the treasury. Many rich people put in large sums. A poor widow also came and put in two small coins worth a few cents. Calling his disciples to himself, he said to them, "Amen, I say to you, this poor widow put in more than all the other contributors to the treasury. For they have all contributed from their surplus wealth, but she, from her poverty, has contributed all she had, her whole livelihood."

— MARK 12:41– 44

My eyes were blinded by the tears that the ugly incident had caused. The richest gifts, the most lavish promises, would have left me unconsoled. Then my two-year-old came up to me, looked at me with mute, sad eyes, and placed her teddy in my lap. It was everything she had. It was everything I needed.

Tobit 12:1, 5–15, 20
Tobit 13:2, 6
Mark 12:38–44

Sunday

JUNE 10

• THE HOLY TRINITY •

[T]he love of God has been poured out into our hearts
through the holy Spirit that has been given to us.

— ROMANS 5:5

What has been poured into us must be
allowed to flow out again to others, lest we
stagnate and die.

Proverbs 8:22–31
Psalm 8
Romans 5:1–5
John 16:12–15

"Blessed are the poor in spirit,
for theirs is the kingdom of heaven."

— MATTHEW 5:3

The first thing she noticed out of the emptiness
following her husband's death was a tiny wild
rose shoot, pushing through the gap
between the paving stones. A flower blooming in
her desert space. A fullness that needed
emptiness in which to grow. An emptied heart,
full of space for the coming of a kingdom.

Acts 11:21–26; 13:1–3
Psalm 98
Matthew 5:1–12

JUNE 12

"You are the salt of the earth. But if salt loses its taste, with
what can it be seasoned? It is no longer good for anything
but to be thrown out and trampled underfoot."

— MATTHEW 5:13

We are called not to add piquancy to our own
private meal, but to let the flavor of God
spread through the whole human stew so that
everyone's appetite is sharpened.

2 Corinthians 1:18–22
Psalm 119
Matthew 5:13–16

"Do not think that I have come to abolish the law or the prophets. I have come not to abolish but to fulfill."

— MATTHEW 5:17

Faithful obedience leads at last to the fullness of love, as surely as the laws received by the children of Israel led to the dawn of resurrection.

2 Corinthians 3:4–11
Psalm 99
Matthew 5:17–19

*Therefore, if you bring your gift to the altar, and there recall that your
brother has anything against you, leave your gift there at the altar,
go first and be reconciled with your brother, and then come and
offer your gift.*

— MATTHEW 5:23 – 24

You could almost see the wall of tension between them as
they sat icily side by side through the first part of the
Eucharist, each brooding bitterly over last night's fight. But
there was no escaping the moment of truth. Eyes lowered,
they reached out reluctant hands. "Peace be with you,"
he muttered. "And peace be with you," she almost choked.
Then their eyes met. Something snapped. Something
changed. Tonight would be different. It was possible to try
again. They went forward together, to receive communion.

2 Corinthians 3:15–4:1, 3–6
Psalm 85
Matthew 5:20–26

But we hold this treasure in earthen vessels, that the surpassing power may be of God and not from us.

— 2 CORINTHIANS 4:7

Even when we are shattered, the worst that
can happen is that God's love and grace
and power spill over into the waiting world.

2 Corinthians 4:7–15
Psalm 116
Matthew 5:27–32

*So whoever is in Christ is a new creation: the old things
have passed away; behold, new things have come. And all
this is from God, who has reconciled us to himself through
Christ and given us the ministry of reconciliation, namely,
God was reconciling the world to himself in Christ, not
counting their trespasses against them and entrusting to us
the message of reconciliation.*

— 2 CORINTHIANS 5:17–19

To see the world as you see it would be a daily
miracle. But you call us to even more than this:
you call us to become the means of sharing
the vision, of multiplying the miracle.

2 Corinthians 5:14–21
Psalm 103
Matthew 5:33–37

Sunday

JUNE 17

*Then taking the five loaves and the two fish, and looking
up to heaven, he said the blessing over them, broke them,
and gave them to the disciples to set before the crowd. They
all ate and were satisfied. And when the leftover fragments
were picked up, they filled twelve wicker baskets.*

— LUKE 9:16 – 17

When our lives feel broken, let us not forget that
you break us only to give us to each other, and
that before ever we are broken, we are blessed.

Genesis 14:18–20
Psalm 110
1 Corinthians 11:23–26
Luke 9:11–17

Monday

JUNE 18

Should anyone press you into service for one mile, go with him for two miles. Give to the one who asks of you, and do not turn your back on one who wants to borrow.

— MATTHEW 5:41 – 42

I simmer inwardly as I force myself to do the chores that life imposes on me. For the first mile I feel like a slave. Yet when the obligation is lifted, I can do exactly the same tasks again, in a free spirit, and discover joy in doing them.
I walk the second mile like a prince.

2 Corinthians 6:1–10
Psalm 98
Matthew 5:38–42

Tuesday

JUNE 19

*But I say to you, love your enemies, and pray for those
who persecute you, that you may be children of your
heavenly Father, for he makes his sun rise on the bad and
the good, and causes rain to fall on the just and the unjust.*

— MATTHEW 5:44 – 45

I need all my energy for living toward your
fullness. The energy I expend in anger and
resentment is diverted and lost. The energy I use
for loving and praying is multiplied. It helps to
neutralize my enemy's destructive feelings, and it
protects me from my own.

2 Corinthians 8:1–9
Psalm 146
Matthew 5:43–48

But when you pray, go to your inner room, close the door,
and pray to your Father in secret. And your Father who
sees in secret will repay you.

— MATTHEW 6:6

The Israelites carried Yahweh with them on their
journeying, in the tabernacle-tent. To pray is to
discover our own tabernacle-tent in the deep
silence of our heart and to enter its secret, sacred
space to meet with the Lord of the journey.

2 Corinthians 9:6–11
Psalm 112
Matthew 6:1–6, 16–18

In praying, do not babble like the pagans, who think that they will be heard because of their many words. Do not be like them. Your Father knows what you need before you ask him.

— MATTHEW 6:7–8

In the excitement of first meeting, the friends hardly stopped talking. But as their friendship deepened, they discovered that their most profound feelings could only be communicated in a receptive silence.

2 Corinthians 11:1–11
Psalm 111
Matthew 6:7–15

The lost I will seek out, the strayed I will bring back, the injured I will bind up, the sick I will heal.

— EZEKIEL 34:16

The lords of the nations exclude the misfits, imprison those who stray, marginalize the wounded, and make the strong even stronger. Lord, that we might learn the wisdom of your ways and the compassion of your heart.

Ezekiel 34:11–16
Psalm 23
Romans 5:5–11
Luke 15:3–7

Saturday

JUNE 23

• THE IMMACULATE HEART OF MARY •

*"My grace is sufficient for you, for power is made
perfect in weakness."*

— 2 CORINTHIANS 12:9

Marion was known throughout the district for
her amazing pastry-making skills. But this
success had not always been there. It had only
come when her fingers became crippled
with arthritis and she was only able to handle
the pastry with the lightest and most
delicate of touches.

2 Corinthians 12:1–10
Psalm 34
Luke 2:41–51

———————————

[A]nd as John was completing his course, he would say, "What do you suppose that I am? I am not he. Behold, one is coming after me; I am not worthy to unfasten the sandals of his feet."

— ACTS 13:25

Give us the grace, Lord, to let our lives become pointers toward you and not destinations in themselves.

VIGIL:
Jeremiah 1:4–10
Psalm 71
1 Peter 1:8–12
Luke 1:5–17

DAY:
Isaiah 49:1–6
Psalm 139
Acts 13:22–26
Luke 1:57–66, 80

"Stop judging, that you may not be judged. For as you judge, so will you be judged, and the measure with which you measure will be measured out to you. Why do you notice the splinter in your brother's eye, but do not perceive the wooden beam in your own eye?"

— MATTHEW 7:1–3

Every time I criticize my friends I alienate them from me a little more; we move further apart, away from the center of warmth and trust that we might have shared. Every time I acknowledge my own shortcomings, instead of exposing theirs, we are drawn closer together into a new understanding and mutual compassion.

Genesis 12:1–9
Psalm 33
Matthew 7:1–5

Now Abram was very rich in livestock, silver, and gold. . . . Lot, who
went with Abram, also had flocks and herds and tents, so that the land
could not support them if they stayed together;
their possessions were so great that they could not dwell together.

— GENESIS 13:2, 5 – 6

Archaeologists tell us that the first general
evidence of murder is linked to the time when people
ceased to be nomadic and started to settle in one
place, accumulate possessions, and envy each
others' treasures. From then on they had too many
possessions to be able to live together.

Genesis 13:2, 5–18
Psalm 15
Matthew 7:6, 12–14

"Beware of false prophets, who come to you in sheep's clothing, but underneath are ravenous wolves. By their fruits you will know them. Do people pick grapes from thornbushes, or figs from thistles? Just so, every good tree bears good fruit, and a rotten tree bears bad fruit."

— MATTHEW 7:15 – 17

Words of reproach, spoken unjustly, yielding resentment. Words of reproach, spoken in love, yielding growth and healing. The fruit reveals the nature of the tree. The harvest identifies the seed.

Genesis 15:1–12, 17–18
Psalm 105
Matthew 7:15–20

Thursday

JUNE 28

• SAINT IRENAEUS, BISHOP AND MARTYR •

"Everyone who listens to these words of mine and acts on them will be like a wise man who built his house on rock. The rain fell, the floods came, and the winds blew and buffeted the house. But it did not collapse; it had been set solidly on rock."

— MATTHEW 7:24–25

It was when I was dashed against the rocks of experience that I discovered the only solid foundation for my life—in the maker of the rocks and the healer of the experience.

Genesis 16:1–12, 15–16 or 16:6–12, 15–16
Psalm 106
Matthew 7:21–29

⋛ 180 ⋜

Friday

JUNE 29

On the very night before Herod was to bring him to trial, Peter, secured by double chains, was sleeping between two soldiers, while outside the door guards kept watch on the prison. Suddenly the angel of the Lord stood by him and a light shone in the cell. He tapped Peter on the side and awakened him, saying, "Get up quickly."
The chains fell from his wrists.

— ACTS 12:6 – 7

Break into the prison of our fears, Lord, and shine the light of your love. With your Word silence the cries of our anxiety. Turn our hearts to you so that the shadow of our fears falls behind us.

VIGIL:	*DAY:*
Acts 3:1–10	Acts 12:1–11
Psalm 19	Psalm 34
Galatians 1:11–20	2 Timothy 4:6–8, 17–18
John 21:15–19	Matthew 16:13–19

*When he entered Capernaum, a centurion approached him and
appealed to him, saying, "Lord, my servant is lying at home paralyzed,
suffering dreadfully." He said to him, "I will come and cure him."
The centurion said in reply, "Lord, I am not worthy to have you enter
under my roof; only say the word and my servant will be healed."*

— MATTHEW 8:5 – 8

The Word that made us, heals us, and lodges eternally
under the roof of our own hearts.

Genesis 18:1–15
Luke 1:46–50, 53–55
Matthew 8:5–17

For freedom Christ set us free; so stand firm and do not submit again to the yoke of slavery.

— GALATIANS 5:1

The vets at the animal shelter worked tirelessly
to free the seabirds from the paralyzing tar
of the oil slick. There would be further disasters,
they knew. But their hearts soared with hope
as they watched the cleansed birds fly free and
high, away above the polluted waters.

1 Kings 19:16, 19–21
Psalm 16
Galatians 5:1, 13–18
Luke 9:51–62

A scribe approached and said to him, "Teacher, I will follow you wherever you go." Jesus answered him, "Foxes have dens and birds of the sky have nests, but the Son of Man has nowhere to rest his head."

— MATTHEW 8:19 – 20

There are moments of desolation when
there is no one, nowhere to turn to,
and every direction seems to lead to despair.
And there, at the still center of the storm,
the homeless One is waiting.

Genesis 18:16—33
Psalm 103
Matthew 8:18—22

Tuesday

JULY 3

• SAINT THOMAS, APOSTLE •

Then he said to Thomas, "Put your finger here and see my
hands, and bring your hand and put it into my side, and
do not be unbelieving, but believe." Thomas answered and
said to him, "My Lord and my God!"

— JOHN 20:27–28

The reality of your living presence is something
far beyond our imagination, Lord, but we begin
to get in touch with it when we have the
courage to touch the world's woundedness with
loving hearts and hands.

Ephesians 2:19–22
Psalm 117
John 20:24–29

Wednesday

JULY 4

• INDEPENDENCE DAY — PROPER MASS IN U.S.A. • SAINT ELIZABETH OF
PORTUGAL •

*When [Jesus] came to the other side, to the territory of the Gadarenes,
two demoniacs who were coming from the tombs met him. They were so
savage that no one could travel by that road. They cried out,
"What have you to do with us, Son of God? Have you come here to
torment us before the appointed time?"*

— MATTHEW 8:28 – 29

I don't know what made me say it. My dark mood took
control of me. My darkness couldn't handle the meeting
with your light and hurled all its strength against you, and
it all came out in a torrent of angry words against my
friend. But your light was even stronger, and my darkness
knew your power and acknowledged its sovereignty.

Genesis 21:5, 8–20
Psalm 34
Matthew 8:28–34

Thursday
JULY 5

• SAINT ANTONY MARY ZACCARIA, PRIEST •

When they came to the place of which God had told him, Abraham built an altar there and arranged the wood on it. Next he tied up his son Isaac, and put him on top of the wood on the altar. Then he reached out and took the knife to slaughter his son. But the LORD's messenger called to him from heaven, "Abraham, Abraham!" "Yes, Lord," he answered. "Do not lay your hand on the boy," said the messenger. "Do not do the least thing to him. I know now how devoted you are to God, since you did not withhold from me your own beloved son."

— GENESIS 22:9–12

Love beyond the limits of all that is reasonable or logical.
Calvary love, taking faith through the eye of the needle
into the possibility of resurrection.

Genesis 22:1–19
Psalm 115
Matthew 9:1–8

The Pharisees saw this and said to his disciples, "Why does your teacher eat with tax collectors and sinners?" He heard this and said, "Those who are well do not need a physician, but the sick do."

— MATTHEW 9:11–12

The sick at heart lie in the streets because they don't recognize the hospital and can't see your healing hands revealed in ours. Strip us, Lord, of our disguises.

Genesis 23:1–4, 19; 24:1–8, 62–67
Psalm 106
Matthew 9:9–13

*"People do not put new wine into old wineskins. Otherwise
the skins burst, the wine spills out, and the skins are ruined.
Rather, they pour new wine into fresh wineskins,
and both are preserved."*

— MATTHEW 9:17

The first moments of life are the most hazardous,
as old and safe containers are left behind to
make space for all that is new. The risk of letting
go is the price of life and growth.

Genesis 27:1–5, 15–29
Psalm 135
Matthew 9:14–17

"I am sending you like lambs among wolves. Carry no money bag, no sack, no sandals; and greet no one along the way. Into whatever house you enter, first say, 'Peace to this household.' If a peaceful person lives there, your peace will rest on him."

— LUKE 10:3 – 6

The mall is milling with Saturday shoppers. Occasionally I look into the face of a passing stranger and her glance meets mine. For a second or two a shaft of recognition passes between us, and we know we have met momentarily in our shared humanity and have been enriched by that meeting as we go our separate ways. Our peace has rested upon each other and been received.

Isaiah 66:10–14
Psalm 66
Galatians 6:14–18
Luke 10:1–12, 17–20 or 10:1–9

When he [Jacob] came upon a certain shrine, as the sun had already set, he stopped there for the night. Taking one of the stones at the shrine, he put it under his head and lay down to sleep at that spot. Then he had a dream: a stairway rested on the ground, with its top reaching to the heavens; and God's messengers were going up and down on it. And there was the LORD standing beside him and saying: "I, the LORD, am the God of your forefather Abraham and the God of Isaac; the land on which you are lying I will give to you and your descendants. These shall be as plentiful as the dust of the earth, and through them you shall spread out east and west, north and south. In you and your descendants all the nations of the earth shall find blessing. Know that I am with you; I will protect you wherever you go, and bring you back to this land. I will never leave you until I have done what I promised you." When Jacob awoke from his sleep, he exclaimed, "Truly, the LORD is in this spot, although I did not know it!"

— GENESIS 28:11–16

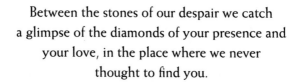

Between the stones of our despair we catch
a glimpse of the diamonds of your presence and
your love, in the place where we never
thought to find you.

Genesis 28:10–22
Psalm 91
Matthew 9:18–26

Keep me as the apple of your eye;
hide me in the shadow of your wings.

— PSALM 17:8

The hidden camera filmed the nest of the newly
hatched owl chicks. Soon there would be flight
and the struggle for survival, but tonight
there was only a warm mound of tawny feathers,
breathing as one. Four chicks completely
enfolded under their mother's wings: source of
love today, and power for flight tomorrow.

Genesis 32:23–33
Psalm 17
Matthew 9:32–38

Wednesday

JULY 11

"Go rather to the lost sheep of the house of Israel. As you go, make this proclamation: 'The kingdom of heaven is at hand.'"

— MATTHEW 10:6 – 7

It was an arduous climb, and the summit seemed to get farther away with every step. Then a fellow walker greeted us: "Not far to go now," he said with a smile. Immediately our steps were lightened, our hearts rejoiced, and our tired trudging became hope-filled again.

Genesis 41:55–57; 42:5–7, 17–24
Psalm 33
Matthew 10:1–7

"*As you go, make this proclamation: 'The kingdom of heaven is at hand.' Cure the sick, raise the dead, cleanse lepers, drive out demons. Without cost you have received; without cost you are to give. Do not take gold or silver or copper for your belts.*"

— MATTHEW 10:7–9

She was old and lonely and lived on her memories. The years of her youth had been given unstintingly to her children and grandchildren. Her love for them was its own reward. Yet how nice it would be if they would find a few minutes to visit her now and again. It would cost so little and mean so much.

Genesis 44:18–21, 23–29; 45:1–5
Psalm 105
Matthew 10:7–15

When they hand you over, do not worry about how you are to speak or what you are to say. You will be given at that moment what you are to say. For it will not be you who speak but the Spirit of your Father speaking through you.

— MATTHEW 10:19 – 20

He was renowned for his talks and lectures, and the hall was packed with people who had come a long way to hear him. A cold shudder ran through him as he realized that he had left his notes at home. He panicked at first but then steadied himself in a few moments of prayerful calm before walking into the auditorium. Afterward they said that it was the best talk he had ever given.

Genesis 46:1–7, 28–30
Psalm 37
Matthew 10:16–23

What I say to you in the darkness, speak in the light;
what you hear whispered, proclaim on the housetops.

— MATTHEW 10:27

What is given in the dark silence of prayer is
for carrying out into the bright lights and clamor
of every day, for the transforming of our
lived experience.

Genesis 49:29–33; 50:15–26
Psalm 105
Matthew 10:24–33

But a Samaritan traveler who came upon him was moved with compassion at the sight. He approached the victim, poured oil and wine over his wounds and bandaged them. Then he lifted him up on his own animal, took him to an inn and cared for him.

— LUKE 10:33 – 34

Jane was the black sheep in high school, with a very dubious reputation. The teachers cold-shouldered her, and her classmates' parents wished she went to some other school. Not many people knew that it was Jane who stopped every evening in the underpass on her way home to share a few words and a sandwich with the homeless people down there.

Deuteronomy 30:10–14
Psalm 69
Colossians 1:15–20
Luke 10:25–37

Monday

JULY 16

• OUR LADY OF MOUNT CARMEL •

We escaped with our lives
like a bird from the fowler's snare;
the snare was broken and we escaped.

— PSALM 124:7

The pet rabbit gnawed away at his hutch until
one day he broke loose. The driver found
him sitting in the middle of the road, hypnotized
by the glare of the lights. Gaining his freedom
had been easy. Living out its consequences and
its potential was altogether harder.

Exodus 1:8–14, 22
Psalm 124
Matthew 10:34–11:1

I have sunk into the mire of the deep,
where there is no foothold.
I have gone down to the watery depths;
the flood overwhelms me.

— PSALM 69:3

At the bottom of the deepest layer of mud there
will be the solid rock that will hold me and let
me fall no further. I know it from my experience.
Why do I always forget it while I am sinking?

Exodus 2:1–15
Psalm 69
Matthew 11:20–24

Wednesday

JULY 18

At that time Jesus said in reply, "I give praise to you,
Father, Lord of heaven and earth, for although you have
hidden these things from the wise and the learned you have
revealed them to the childlike."

— MATTHEW 11:25

We still had three miles to walk, and we
had promised to be home for lunch. Our toddler
suddenly sat down in the meadow, gazing
in rapture at the ambling journey of a shiny black
beetle. She was seeing the very first beetle with
the very first eyes—seeing it as you see it.
For a moment we forgot our haste, and then
we saw it too.

Exodus 3:1–6, 9–12
Psalm 103
Matthew 11:25–27

*"Come to me, all you who labor and are burdened, and I
will give you rest. Take my yoke upon you and learn from
me, for I am meek and humble of heart; and you will
find rest for yourselves. For my yoke is easy, and
my burden light."*

— MATTHEW 11:28 – 30

The Palestinian woman lifted the huge weight of
the filled water jug onto her head. An impossible
burden, I thought. Impossible for me,
but she was walking in perfect balance, and
that made her burden light.

Exodus 3:13–20
Psalm 105
Matthew 11:28–30

"This is how you are to eat it: with your loins girt,
sandals on your feet and your staff in hand, you shall eat
like those who are in flight. It is the Passover of the LORD."

— EXODUS 12:11

The journey is unfinished, and you
call us, your Passover people, to be always
ready for the road ahead, every communion
with you a preparation for moving on.

Exodus 11:10–12:14
Psalm 116
Matthew 12:1–8

• SAINT LAWRENCE OF BRINDISI, PRIEST AND DOCTOR OF THE CHURCH •

"Behold, my servant whom I have chosen,
my beloved in whom I delight;
I shall place my spirit upon him,
and he will proclaim justice to the Gentiles.
He will not contend or cry out,
nor will anyone hear his voice in the streets."

— MATTHEW 12:18 – 19

Your voice speaks to us in the silence, and in
your silent presence within us we proclaim that
presence to everyone we meet.

Exodus 12:37–42
Psalm 136
Matthew 12:14–21

Sunday

JULY 22

Martha, burdened with much serving, came to him and said, "Lord, do you not care that my sister has left me by myself to do the serving? Tell her to help me." The Lord said to her in reply, "Martha, Martha, you are anxious and worried about many things. There is need of only one thing. Mary has chosen the better part and it will not be taken from her."

— LUKE 10:40 – 42

The church parlor was full of notices: a garden party, a list
of cleaning volunteers, coffee mornings and discussion
groups, hospital visiting, and mother-and-toddler groups.
A lively church. And in a small side chapel there was
the most important notice of all: "Reserved for quiet prayer."

Genesis 18:1–10
Psalm 15
Colossians 1:24–28
Luke 10:38–42

Monday

J U L Y 2 3

*But Moses answered the people, "Fear not! Stand your
ground, and you will see the victory the LORD will win for
you today. These Egyptians whom you see today you will
never see again. The LORD himself will fight for you;
you have only to keep still."*

— EXODUS 14:13 – 14

The lifeguard could do nothing until the victim
stopped struggling and fell into unconsciousness.
From then on it was easy to draw him gently but
firmly to the shore. Give us the grace, Lord, to
trust in your strength more than in our own
efforts, and to stop getting in the way of your
saving power.

Exodus 14:5–18
Exodus 15:1–6
Matthew 12:38–42

And you brought them in and planted them
on the mountain of your inheritance—
the place where you made your seat, O LORD,
the sanctuary, O LORD, which your hands established.

— EXODUS 15:17

Jason watched over the seedlings in his
greenhouse with loving devotion. One by one,
when the time was right, he planted them in
their permanent place in his garden—in a special
place that he had chosen and prepared
for each one of them, a place where they would
be forever a part of his home.

Exodus 14:21–15:1
Exodus 15:8–10, 12, 17
Matthew 12:46–50

Wednesday

JULY 25

• SAINT JAMES, APOSTLE •

Then the mother of the sons of Zebedee approached him
with her sons and did him homage, wishing to ask him for
something. He said to her, "What do you wish?" She
answered him, "Command that these two sons of mine sit,
one at your right and the other at your left, in your
kingdom." Jesus said in reply, "You do not know what
you are asking. Can you drink the cup that I am
going to drink?"

— MATTHEW 20:20 – 22

Among my friends I often notice that those who
have drunk most deeply of the cup of suffering
are the ones whose lives seem closest to you.

2 Corinthians 4:7–15
Psalm 126
Matthew 20:20–28

Whenever the cloud rose from the Dwelling, the Israelites would set out on their journey. But if the cloud did not lift, they would not go forward; only when it lifted did they go forward. In the daytime the cloud of the LORD was seen over the Dwelling; whereas at night, fire was seen in the cloud by the whole house of Israel in all the stages of their journey.

— EXODUS 40:36 – 38

The clouds are down so often, and I seem to spend much more of my life in waiting than in marching. But I know from experience that they will lift eventually and I will move on, because that has been so for every stage of my journey, and I trust it for the remainder.

Exodus 19:1–2, 9–11, 16–20
Psalm 132
Matthew 13:10–17

*He came to his native place and taught the people in their
synagogue. They were astonished and said, "Where did
this man get such wisdom and mighty deeds? Is he not the
carpenter's son?"*

— MATTHEW 13:54 – 55

She was a nonentity in the village. She was John's
wife and Sally's mother, the doctor's daughter
and the school's secretary. Then she met
a friend who called her by her name and knew
her for herself, and who released all her unique
potential. And the villagers were amazed.

Exodus 20:1–17
Psalm 19
Matthew 13:18–23

But at a birthday celebration for Herod, the daughter of Herodias performed a dance before the guests and delighted Herod so much that he swore to give her whatever she might ask for. Prompted by her mother, she said, "Give me here on a platter the head of John the Baptist." The king was distressed, but because of his oaths and the guests who were present, he ordered that it be given, and he had John beheaded in the prison.

— MATTHEW 14:6–10

He had had too much to drink and was in no mood to be coaxed home by his embarrassed wife. Instead he told a crude story against her. His pride was saved, but something irreplaceable was lost that evening.

Exodus 24:3–8
Psalm 50
Matthew 13:24–30

"What father among you would hand his son a snake when he asks for a fish? Or hand him a scorpion when he asks for an egg? If you then, who are wicked, know how to give good gifts to your children, how much more will the Father in heaven give the holy Spirit to those who ask him?"

— LUKE 11:11 – 13

Alice was dying before her time, in a makeshift hospital ward at the end of the war. A minor operation had gone wrong because she was so seriously undernourished and weak. Yet there was joy in her eyes as she held her little grandson in her arms. Then she pressed a small paper bag into his hands—her month's sugar ration and her only source of energy. Small token of immeasurable love.

Genesis 18:20–32
Psalm 138
Colossians 2:12–24
Luke 11:1–13

JULY 30

> [T]hey fashioned a calf,
> worshiped a metal statue.
> They exchanged their glorious God
> for the image of a grass-eating bull.
> — PSALM 106:19 – 20

James was a self-made man. He had a successful
career, a well-organized family, and a tidy,
prosperous lifestyle. Self-made, from head to
toe, but unable to face the empty space where
God had intended his heart to be.

Exodus 32:15–24, 30–34
Psalm 106
Matthew 13:31–35

Tuesday

JULY 31

• SAINT IGNATIUS OF LOYOLA, PRIEST •

Moses at once bowed down to the ground in worship. Then
he said, "If I find favor with you, O LORD, do come along
in our company. This is indeed a stiff-necked people;
yet pardon our wickedness and sins, and receive
us as your own."

— EXODUS 34:8 – 9

You have walked with me down every cul-de-sac
into which my willfulness has led me, waiting
for your headstrong child to find her destination
in the One who walks beside her.

Exodus 33:7–11; 34:5–9, 28
Psalm 103
Matthew 13:35–43

AUGUST 1

• SAINT ALPHONSUS LIGUORI, BISHOP AND DOCTOR OF THE CHURCH •

*Whenever Moses entered the presence of the LORD to
converse with him, he removed the veil until he came out
again. On coming out, he would tell the Israelites all that
had been commanded. Then the Israelites would see that the
skin of Moses' face was radiant.*

— EXODUS 34:34 – 35

Martin was a person of prayer. Though he never
said so, you could see it in his eyes and hear it
in the quiet authority with which he shared what
he had heard in the darkness.

Exodus 34:29–35
Psalm 99
Matthew 13:44–46

Thursday

AUGUST 2

And he [Jesus] replied, "Then every scribe who has been instructed in the kingdom of heaven is like the head of a household who brings from his storeroom both the new and the old."

— MATTHEW 13:52

The freshness of my life's stream flows boldly through every day's new landscape, but it flows out of old, almost forgotten sources.

Exodus 40:16–21, 34–38
Psalm 84
Matthew 13:47–53

"*When you come into the land which I am giving you, and reap your harvest, you shall bring a sheaf of the first fruits of your harvest to the priest, who shall wave the sheaf before the LORD.*"

— LEVITICUS 23:10 – 11

You give me all the gifts of my life, and to you I return them, for you know far better than I how they might best be used.

Leviticus 23:1, 4–11, 15–16, 27, 34–37
Psalm 81
Matthew 13:54–58

⇒ 217 ⇐

May God be gracious to us and bless us;
may God's face shine upon us.

— PSALM 67:2

The ward sister was exhausted after the long,
demanding night shift. She stopped by
Jane's bedside and noticed that she had, at last,
sunk into peaceful sleep. And then the
first shaft of dawn came slanting down through
the window, as if to add your blessing to
the long night's ending.

Leviticus 25:1, 8–17
Psalm 67
Matthew 14:1–12

*Then he [Jesus] said to the crowd, "Take care to guard against all greed,
for though one may be rich, one's life does not consist of possessions."*

— LUKE 12:15

The Neighborhood Watch meeting had just heard the
police talk on household security systems. The next
morning Joe noticed that May hadn't taken in her morning
paper. A signal for burglars, he thought, and went
round to check on her. It was then that he found her
lying helpless, after her fall. And it was then that
he learned that neighborly watchfulness is about a different
kind of security.

Ecclesiastes 1:2, 2:21–23
Psalm 95
Colossians 3:1–5, 9–11
Luke 12:13–21

*[H]e [Jesus] took Peter, John, and James and went up the
mountain to pray. While he was praying his face changed
in appearance and his clothing became dazzling white.*

— LUKE 9:28 – 29

When the thick layers of our self-defense and
self-importance fall away, then at last the
flickering flame of faith in our hearts will shine
free, transfiguring us into the carriers of your
radiant love.

Daniel 7:9–10, 13–14
Psalm 97
2 Peter 1:16–19
Luke 9:28–36

Tuesday

AUGUST 7

• SAINT SIXTUS II, POPE AND MARTYR, AND HIS COMPANIONS, MARTYRS •
• SAINT CAJETAN, PRIEST •

*During the fourth watch of the night, he came toward them,
walking on the sea. When the disciples saw him walking on the sea they
were terrified. "It is a ghost," they said, and they cried out in fear.
At once [Jesus] spoke to them, "Take courage, it is I; do not be afraid."
Peter said to him in reply, "Lord, if it is you, command me to
come to you on the water." He said, "Come." Peter got out of the boat
and began to walk on the water toward Jesus. But when he saw
how (strong) the wind was he became frightened; and, beginning to sink,
he cried out, "Lord, save me!"*

— MATTHEW 14:25 – 30

Philip was well in the lead and seemed certain to win the race. All his energy was focused on that one supreme goal.

Then there was a disturbance among the spectators. He glanced sideways at the crowd, suddenly conscious of his surroundings and their dangers. From that moment his focus was lost, and so was the race.

Numbers 12:1–13
Psalm 51
Matthew 14:22–36

Wednesday

AUGUST 8

*After reconnoitering the land for forty days they returned, met Moses
and Aaron and the whole community of the Israelites in the desert of
Paran at Kadesh, made a report to them all, and showed them the fruit of
the country. They told Moses: "We went into the land to which you sent
us. It does indeed flow with milk and honey, and here is its fruit.
However, the people who are living in the land are fierce, and the towns
are fortified and very strong."*

— NUMBERS 13:25 – 28

Just when I begin to taste the joy of the milk and
the honey, I come face-to-face with one of the powerful
giants of fear, or doubt, or pride, who populate
my inner kingdom. The honey of your promise is not
drawn from a bed of roses.

Numbers 13:1–2, 25–14:1, 26–29, 34–35
Psalm 106
Matthew 15:21–28

⇒ 223 ⇐

[T]he LORD said to Moses, "Take the staff and assemble
the community, you and your brother Aaron, and in their
presence order the rock to yield its waters. From the rock
you shall bring forth water for the community and their
livestock to drink."

— NUMBERS 20:7–8

The hard immovable rocks of our lives
sometimes prove to be the hidden, unsuspected
sources of your greatest gifts to us, if we
only have the courage and the trust to face
them in faith.

Numbers 20:1–13
Psalm 95
Matthew 16:13–23

*Then Jesus said to his disciples, "Whoever wishes to come
after me must deny himself, take up his cross, and follow
me. For whoever wishes to save his life will lose it, but
whoever loses his life for my sake will find it."*

— MATTHEW 16:24 – 25

The less there is of me, the more space there is
for you. And the more I let you fill me, the more
completely I become who I really am.

2 Corinthians 9:6–10
Psalm 112
John 12:24–26

"Hear, O Israel! The LORD is our God, the LORD alone! Therefore, you shall love the LORD, your God, with all your heart, and with all your soul, and with all your strength. Take to heart these words which I enjoin on you today. Drill them into your children. Speak of them at home and abroad, whether you are busy or at rest. Bind them at your wrist as a sign and let them be as a pendant on your forehead. Write them on the doorposts of your houses and on your gates."

— DEUTERONOMY 6:4 – 9

Sue and David's home is always open. All sorts of people seek them out and find a welcome there. If you could see into the deep recesses of their being, you would find these words inscribed on the doorposts of their hearts: "God lives here."

Deuteronomy 6:4–13
Psalm 18
Matthew 17:14–20

*Do not be afraid any longer, little flock, for your Father is
pleased to give you the kingdom.*

— LUKE 12:32

Julie flopped into the chair, so thankful for the
relaxing acceptance of her friend's home
after a grueling day of trying to make a good
impression at the job interview. Here there
was nothing to fear. Her friend gave her freely
the love and affirmation that she had been
striving so hard and so fruitlessly to earn for
herself in the workplace.

Wisdom 18:6–9
Psalm 33
Hebrews 11:1–2, 8–19 or 11:1–2, 8–12
Luke 12:32–48 or 12:35–40

AUGUST 13

• SAINTS PONTIAN, POPE AND MARTYR, AND HIPPOLYTUS, PRIEST AND MARTYR •

So you too must befriend the alien, for you were once aliens yourselves in the land of Egypt.

— DEUTERONOMY 10:19

The children stood round in a huddle and stared at the newcomer as he trailed shyly, fearfully, across the playground. It was Martin who broke the wall of tension with a friendly word for the frightened stranger. Martin had been new here himself last term.

Deuteronomy 10:12–22
Psalm 147
Matthew 17:22–27

*He called a child over, placed it in their midst, and said,
"Amen, I say to you, unless you turn and become like
children, you will not enter the kingdom of heaven.
Whoever humbles himself like this child is the greatest
in the kingdom of heaven."*

— MATTHEW 18:2 – 4

The Reception Class is well named. It is not only
the place for those who are to be received into
the church but also for those who, of all people,
are the ones most receptive to the wonders
that lie around them, waiting for discovery.

Deuteronomy 31:1–8
Deuteronomy 32:3–4, 7, 8, 9, 12
Matthew 18:1–5, 10, 12–14

[F]rom now on will all ages call me blessed.
The Mighty One has done great things for me,
and holy is his name.
His mercy is from age to age
to those who fear him.

— LUKE 1:48 – 50

When just one of your children acknowledges
your holiness from her heart, a spring of
blessing is opened up, which will cascade down
through the generations to come.

VIGIL:
1 Chronicles 15:3–4, 15–16; 16:1–2
Psalm 132
1 Corinthians 15:54–57
Luke 11:27–28

DAY:
Revelation 11:19; 12:1–6, 10
Psalm 45
1 Corinthians 15:20–27
Luke 1:39–56

So Joshua said to the Israelites, "Come here and listen to
the words of the LORD, your God." He continued:
"This is how you will know that there is a living God
in your midst."

— JOSHUA 3:9 – 10

Jane's correspondence with her pen pal had been,
necessarily, a little forced and stilted. But when
they finally met and stayed in each other's
homes, their paper connection changed into a
living relationship that was a source of richness
and joy to them both. Help us to change
our long-distance acquaintance with you into the
close and living encounter you long for it to be.

Joshua 3:7–11, 13–17
Psalm 114
Matthew 18:21–19:1

"I gave you a land which you had not tilled and cities which you had not built, to dwell in; you have eaten of vineyards and olive groves which you did not plant."

— JOSHUA 24:13

Maureen used her parents' home like a hotel and frequently filled it with her teenage friends. She seemed to have no appreciation of all that they had put into creating a home for her. Then one night she flung her arms round her parents' necks and hugged them. Nothing was said, but at that moment they realized that the seeds they had sown had taken root in her heart and would yield their own fruits in a home that she herself would one day create for children yet unborn.

Joshua 24:1–13
Psalm 136
Matthew 19:3–12

AUGUST 18

*Then children were brought to him that he might lay his
hands on them and pray. The disciples rebuked them, but
Jesus said, "Let the children come to me, and do not prevent
them; for the kingdom of heaven belongs
to such as these."*

— MATTHEW 19:13 – 14

Carol's kitchen was always full of children. No
one was ever sent away. Among them were those
who found no such welcome in their own
cold homes and who flocked to Carol for their
warming. Probably she never realized how
perfectly she was carrying out your command.

Joshua 24:14—29
Psalm 16
Matthew 19:13—15

Therefore, since we are surrounded by so great a cloud of witnesses, let us rid ourselves of every burden and sin that clings to us and persevere in running the race that lies before us while keeping our eyes fixed on Jesus, the leader and perfecter of faith.

— HEBREWS 12:1–2

I stand in line, waiting to receive communion. For a moment I see myself standing in another, longer line. In front of me are all those who have gone before, in faith. Behind me are all who will follow after. And at our head, the source and destination of our journey, is the Christ who leads and waits to be received.

Jeremiah 38:4–6, 8–10
Psalm 40
Hebrews 12:1–4
Luke 12:49–53

———

Monday

AUGUST 20

• SAINT BERNARD, ABBOT AND DOCTOR OF THE CHURCH •

*The young man said to him, "All of these I have observed.
What do I still lack?" Jesus said to him, "If you wish
to be perfect, go, sell what you have and give to (the) poor,
and you will have treasure in heaven. Then come,
follow me."*

— MATTHEW 19:20 – 21

You are a tenant of my heart, sharing its space
with so many lesser lodgers. Become its owner
and its whole possessor, Lord, for only when
there is no room for any other, then there will be
infinity for all.

Judges 2:11–19
Psalm 106
Matthew 19:16–22

*Then Jesus said to his disciples, "Amen, I say to you, it
will be hard for one who is rich to enter the kingdom of
heaven. Again I say to you, it is easier for a camel
to pass through the eye of a needle than for one who is rich
to enter the kingdom of God."*

— MATTHEW 19:23 – 24

When I let go of my need to possess and
I surrender to the emptiness of the
needle's eye, I stand on the threshold of
an unimaginable fullness.

Judges 6:11–24
Psalm 85
Matthew 19:23–30

"Thus, the last will be first, and the first will be last."
— MATTHEW 20:16

In your human life, Lord, you were usually at the
end of the world's lines, among the rejects and
outcasts of society. Why, then, am I so anxious
to be at the front of life's lines, among the
achievers and succeeders? Please give me the
grace to let you love me in my failures.

Judges 9:6–15
Psalm 21
Matthew 20:1–16

———————————

[S]acrifice and offering you do not want;
but ears open to obedience you gave me.
Holocausts and sin offerings you do not require;
so I said, "Here I am."

— PSALM 40:6 – 7

Emily was the envy of her classmates. She had
everything a teenager could wish for. Her
parents worked from morning till night to buy
her all she could desire. Jenny had nothing—
except a mom and dad who were there for her
and listened to her dreams.

Judges 11:29–39
Psalm 40
Matthew 22:1–14

Philip found Nathanael and told him, "We have found
the one about whom Moses wrote in the law, and
also the prophets, Jesus, son of Joseph, from Nazareth."
But Nathanael said to him, "Can anything good
come from Nazareth?"

— JOHN 1:45 – 46

We may reject the gift we most long for
because we can't see beyond the packaging it
is wrapped in.

Revelation 21:9–14
Psalm 145
John 1:45–51

The greatest among you must be your servant. Whoever exalts himself will be humbled; but whoever humbles himself will be exalted.

— MATTHEW 23:11–12

After the accident, the principal summoned the school together and gave them an impressive lecture on the dangers of running in the corridors and the importance of dignified behavior. Meanwhile one of the other adults was quietly wiping David's tears away and gently bathing his cut knee.

Ruth 2:1–3, 8–11; 4:13–17
Psalm 128
Matthew 23:1–12

"And people will come from the east and the west and from the north and the south and will recline at table in the kingdom of God. For behold, some are last who will be first, and some are first who will be last."

— LUKE 13:29 – 30

When I finally stopped walking away from you and turned round to face you, I discovered that all my values turned with me and my life was back to front.

Isaiah 66:18–21
Psalm 117
Hebrews 12:5–7, 11–13
Luke 13:22–30

For our gospel did not come to you in word alone, but also in power and in the holy Spirit and (with) much conviction.

— 1 THESSALONIANS 1:5

The Word that inspires us is the Word who created us and the Word who empowers us to become ourselves a word for others.

1 Thessalonians 1:1–5, 8–10
Psalm 149
Matthew 23:13–22

Tuesday

AUGUST 28

• SAINT AUGUSTINE, BISHOP AND DOCTOR OF THE CHURCH •

LORD, you have probed me, you know me:
you know when I sit and stand;
you understand my thoughts from afar.

— PSALM 139:1 – 2

Like a shy and secret bird, I try to conceal
myself from your knowledge of me. Yet hear my
muted prayer-song, Lord. It is my call to you,
to know me in spite of my concealment.

1 Thessalonians 2:1–8
Psalm 139
Matthew 23:23–26

⇒ 243 ⇐

*Herodias's own daughter came in and performed
a dance that delighted Herod and his guests. The king said
to the girl, "Ask of me whatever you wish and I
will grant it to you." He even swore (many things) to her,
"I will grant you whatever you ask of me, even to
half of my kingdom." She went out and said to her mother,
"What shall I ask for?" She replied, "The head of
John the Baptist."*

— MARK 6:22 – 24

When we barter our integrity for pride
and image, we deal death to ourselves and
to the world.

1 Thessalonians 2:9–13
Psalm 71
Mark 6:17–29

*Therefore, stay awake! For you do not know on which day
your Lord will come. . . . So too, you also must be
prepared, for at an hour you do not expect, the
Son of Man will come.*

— MATTHEW 24:42, 44

It was a bleak January day up on the high moors,
and the snow-laden clouds seemed uniformly
gray. Then, just for a moment, the sun broke
through the cloud cover and the hills were
transfigured with light. The vision was over in a
few seconds, but it was enough to sustain us
through a long, cold, winter walk.

1 Thessalonians 3:7–13
Psalm 90
Matthew 24:42–51

"Then the kingdom of heaven will be like ten virgins who took their lamps and went out to meet the bridegroom. Five of them were foolish and five were wise. . . . While they went off to buy [oil], the bridegroom came and those who were ready went into the wedding feast with him. Then the door was locked. Afterwards the other virgins came and said, 'Lord, Lord, open the door for us!' But he said in reply, 'Amen, I say to you, I do not know you.' Therefore, stay awake, for you know neither the day nor the hour."

— MATTHEW 25:1 – 2, 10 – 13

Your surprises catch us up in their joy. Yet how easily we miss them among the clouds of our distractions and preoccupations, and never even realize the value of what we have lost.

1 Thessalonians 4:1–8
Psalm 97
Matthew 25:1–13

"It will be as when a man who was going on a journey called in
his servants and entrusted his possessions to them. To one he gave five
talents; to another, two; to a third, one—to each according to
his ability. Then he went away. Immediately the one who received five
talents went and traded with them, and made another five.
Likewise, the one who received two made another two. But the man who
received one went off and dug a hole in the ground and
buried his master's money."

— MATTHEW 25:14–18

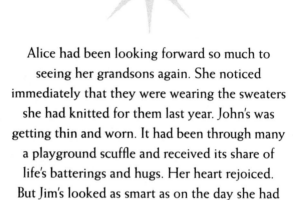

Alice had been looking forward so much to
seeing her grandsons again. She noticed
immediately that they were wearing the sweaters
she had knitted for them last year. John's was
getting thin and worn. It had been through many
a playground scuffle and received its share of
life's batterings and hugs. Her heart rejoiced.
But Jim's looked as smart as on the day she had
given it to him. Barely worn, she thought.
And her heart sank.

1 Thessalonians 4:9–11
Psalm 98
Matthew 25:14–30

Father of the fatherless, defender of widows—
this is the God whose abode is holy,
Who gives a home to the forsaken,
who leads prisoners out to prosperity.

— PSALM 68:6 – 7

First we discover in you everything we truly are.
And then the even greater discoveries begin
as we find in you everything we lack and long for.

Sirach 3:17–18, 20, 28–29
Psalm 68
Hebrews 12:18–19, 22–24
Luke 14:1, 7–14

Monday

SEPTEMBER 3

• LABOR DAY • SAINT GREGORY THE GREAT, POPE AND DOCTOR OF THE CHURCH •

*"The Spirit of the Lord is upon me,
because he has anointed me
to bring glad tidings to the poor.
He has sent me to proclaim liberty to captives
and recovery of sight to the blind,
to let the oppressed go free, and to proclaim a year
acceptable to the Lord."
Rolling up the scroll, [Jesus] handed it back to the
attendant and sat down, and the eyes of all in the synagogue
looked intently at him. He said to them, "Today this scripture
passage is fulfilled in your hearing."*

— LUKE 4:17 – 21

I walked through the upscale estate and
wondered about its inhabitants. I thought of
words that spoke of the poor, encased in wealth
yet starved of love, and of captives who
have purchased every luxury and have had
to fence themselves in to defend it. These, too,
are your poor, blind, and oppressed, and
claimants on your love.

1 Thessalonians 4:13–18
Psalm 96
Luke 4:16–30

SEPTEMBER 4

But I believe I shall enjoy the LORD's goodness
in the land of the living.
Wait for the LORD, take courage;
be stouthearted, wait for the LORD!

— PSALM 27:13 – 14

There was nothing meaningful she could do to
reach him in his despair. All she could offer
was a hand on his shoulder, with the words, "Let
me carry the hope for you until you are
strong enough to pick it up again for yourself."

1 Thessalonians 5:1–6, 9–11
Psalm 27
Luke 4:31–37

But I, like an olive tree in the house of God,
trust in God's faithful love forever.

— PSALM 52:10

Like seeds we are called to growth, trusting in
the unseen goodness of the soil that holds us,
called to yield fruits for the nourishing of many.

Colossians 1:1–8
Psalm 52
Luke 4:38–44

He [Jesus] saw two boats there alongside the lake; the
fishermen had disembarked and were washing their
nets. . . . and likewise James and John, the sons of
Zebedee, who were partners of Simon. Jesus said to Simon,
"Do not be afraid; from now on you will be catching men."

— LUKE 5:2,10

The love of God is caught, not taught, and we
are called to be the source of the contagion.

Colossians 1:9–14
Psalm 98
Luke 5:1–11

Friday

SEPTEMBER 7

He is the image of the invisible God,
the firstborn of all creation.
For in him were created all things in heaven and on earth.
— COLOSSIANS 1:15 – 16

Everywhere I look, in every part of your
creation, I see your face in what you
have created, each image reflecting that special
aspect of your nature that it alone can reflect.

Colossians 1:15–20
Psalm 100
Luke 5:33–39

But you, Bethlehem-Ephrathah,
too small to be among the clans of Judah,
From you shall come forth for me
one who is to be ruler in Israel.

— MICAH 5:1

We may wait in vain for growth
and renewal in the center of our societies and
institutions, while all the while the transforming
changes are happening on the margins,
among the dispossessed and powerless, and in
the poorest peoples.

Micah 5:1–4 or Romans 8:28–30
Psalm 13
Matthew 1:1–16, 18–23 or 1:18–23

———————

[Y]ou have brought them to their end;
They disappear like sleep at dawn;
they are like grass that dies.
It sprouts green in the morning;
by evening it is dry and withered.

— PSALM 90:5 – 6

As we watch the chicks of May take flight
on their autumn migrations—hatched yesterday
and flown tomorrow—we remember our
own springing and fading, and we trust you
for the unseen harvest.

Wisdom 9:13–18
Psalm 90
Philemon 9–10, 12–17
Luke 14:25–33

SEPTEMBER 10

*Now I rejoice in my sufferings for your sake, and in my
flesh I am filling up what is lacking in the afflictions of
Christ on behalf of his body, which is the church.*

— COLOSSIANS 1:24

Judith endures chronic pain and immobility.
It could have hardened her heart into bitterness.
Instead she consciously joins it to the pain
of Gethsemane and Calvary, living out in her
own time and place the struggle and the
power of the cross. It has softened her heart into
a tenderness that flows over into every other
heart that it encounters.

Colossians 1:24–2:3
Psalm 62
Luke 6:6–11

*And he came down with them and stood on a stretch of
level ground. A great crowd of his disciples and a large
number of the people. . . . Everyone in the crowd sought to
touch him because power came forth from him and
healed them all.*

— LUKE 6:17–19

You do not call us to climb mountains in your
name or to stand on the pinnacles of
achievement. Instead you invite us to come
down, humbly, to the level ground, where
your people wait and hope and trust. You invite
us only to be there, carrying you in our hearts,
trusting in your healing power, for us and for all.

Colossians 2:6–15
Psalm 145
Luke 6:12–19

For you have died, and your life is hidden with Christ in
God. When Christ your life appears, then you too will
appear with him in glory.

— COLOSSIANS 3:3 – 4

Our daffodil bulbs can have no idea of what they
will become next April. But we, who have
planted them in the darkness, we know what
glory lies hidden in their hearts, and we
rejoice in the joy and trust of anticipation.

Colossians 3:1–11
Psalm 145
Luke 6:20–26

Thursday

SEPTEMBER 13

• SAINT JOHN CHRYSOSTOM, BISHOP AND DOCTOR OF THE CHURCH •

*"But to you who hear I say, love your enemies, do good to
those who hate you, bless those who curse you, pray for
those who mistreat you."*

— LUKE 6:27–28

When I disarm my enemy with a smile, I achieve
far more than when I arm myself with
sarcasm and disdain. Something negative is
prevented and reversed, and one little
arrow of pain is rendered harmless.

Colossians 3:12–17
Psalm 150
Luke 6:27–38

For God did not send his Son into the world to condemn the
world, but that the world might be saved through him.

— JOHN 3:17

Each thought or word of judgment undermines
your kingdom, Lord. Every gesture of affirmation
and encouragement builds it up.

Numbers 21:4–9
Psalm 78
Philippians 2:6–11
John 3:13–17

Simeon blessed them and said to Mary his mother, "Behold, this child is destined for the fall and rise of many in Israel, and to be a sign that will be contradicted (and you yourself a sword will pierce) so that the thoughts of many hearts may be revealed."

— LUKE 2:34 – 35

The sword of truth may strip me of all my disguises and defenses. When this happens, dare I look into the mirror you place before me, and see who I really am? And dare I let you love the "me" I see?

1 Timothy 1:15–17
Psalm 31
John 19:25–27 or Luke 2:33–35

Sunday

SEPTEMBER 16

With that, the LORD said to Moses, "Go down at once to your
people . . . They [are] . . . making for themselves a molten calf and
worshiping it . . . Let me alone, then, that my wrath may blaze up
against them to consume them. Then I will make of you a great nation."
But Moses implored the LORD, his God, saying, "Why, O LORD,
should your wrath blaze up against your own people . . . ?" So the
LORD relented.

— EXODUS 32:7–11,14

Janet and Jean huddled together, terrified by their mother's
fury. The damage was entirely Jean's fault. Janet went to
their mother and begged her not to punish Jean. Her mother
looked at them and saw in Janet's eyes a depth of love
for her sister that took her completely by surprise.
It was more than strong enough to overcome her rage.

Exodus 32:7–11, 13–14
Psalm 51
1 Timothy 1:12–17
Luke 15:1–32 or 15:1–10

Monday

SEPTEMBER 17

• SAINT ROBERT BELLARMINE, BISHOP AND DOCTOR OF THE CHURCH •

The LORD is my strength and my shield,
in whom my heart trusted and found help.

— PSALM 28:7

How strong is my trust in you, Lord? Weaker
than the power of my greatest fear! But you
are asking me to trust that your power is greater
than the combined force of all my fears,
all the world's fears. And such trust is possible,
because you have pinned it on the cross for
all to see and share.

1 Timothy 2:1–8
Psalm 28
Luke 7:1–10

≥ 265 ≤

Tuesday

SEPTEMBER 18

As he drew near to the gate of the city, a man who had died was being carried out, the only son of his mother, and she was a widow. . . . When the Lord saw her, he was moved with pity for her and said to her, "Do not weep." He stepped forward and touched the coffin; at this the bearers halted, and he said, "Young man, I tell you, arise!" The dead man sat up and began to speak, and Jesus gave him to his mother.

— LUKE 7:12 – 15

The miracle of healing begins with compassion and leads to the giving back of life. Give us compassion for each other, Lord, that we too may restore each other to the fullness of life.

1 Timothy 3:1–13
Psalm 101
Luke 7:11–17

Undeniably great is the mystery of devotion.

—1 TIMOTHY 3:16

Your nature is a mystery infinitely beyond our
understanding, yet like life itself, it is revealed in
everyone we meet, in everything we experience,
in every stirring of our deepest hearts.

1 Timothy 3:14–16
Psalm 111
Luke 7:31–35

• SAINT ANDREW KIM, PRIEST AND MARTYR • SAINT PAUL CHONG HASANG,
CATECHIST AND MARTYR, AND THEIR COMPANIONS, MARTYRS •

Let no one have contempt for your youth, but set an
example for those who believe, in speech, conduct, love,
faith, and purity.

— 1 TIMOTHY 4:12

Nothing would persuade Christopher to go to
church with his parents. He just couldn't see the
point. But while they were out he called his
friend, Mark, who was in trouble with the police.
There wasn't much he could say, but he
could listen, and understand, and offer the solid
rock of his own integrity for Mark to lean
on for a while.

1 Timothy 4:12–16
Psalm 111
Luke 7:36–50

The Pharisees saw this and said to his disciples, "Why does your teacher eat with tax collectors and sinners?" He heard this and said, "Those who are well do not need a physician, but the sick do."

— MATTHEW 9:11–12

The doctor we need is the one who comes to us where we are and who then sends us to be with others where they are.

Ephesians 4:1–7, 11–13
Psalm 19
Matthew 9:9–13

Saturday

SEPTEMBER 22

*"A sower went out to sow his seed. And as he sowed, some seed
fell on the path and was trampled, and the birds of the sky ate it up.
Some seed fell on rocky ground, and when it grew, it withered for
lack of moisture. Some seed fell among thorns, and the thorns grew with
it and choked it. And some seed fell on good soil, and when it grew,
it produced fruit a hundredfold."*

— LUKE 8:5 – 8

Sometimes the seed of your truth falls onto my soil, my
Friend. But I feel threatened by it and trample it to death.
Or I receive it with a stony silence and deprive it of
life-giving encouragement. Or I crowd it out with my own
concerns and ideas and choke it. Forgive me, my
Friend. Give me the grace to give your seed the space
for growth and fruitfulness.

1 Timothy 6:13–16
Psalm 100
Luke 8:4–15

Sunday

SEPTEMBER 23

We will diminish the ephah,
add to the shekel,
and fix our scales for cheating!
We will buy the lowly man for silver,
and the poor man for a pair of sandals.

— AMOS 8:5 – 6

Whenever I make use of another person's good
nature to achieve my own ends or to bolster
my comfort and ease, I offend against your love
as surely and as seriously as the most
scheming of politicians.

Amos 8:4–7
Psalm 113
1 Timothy 2:1–8
Luke 16:1–13 or 16:10–13

Those who sow in tears
will reap with cries of joy.
Those who go forth weeping,
carrying sacks of seed,
Will return with cries of joy,
carrying their bundled sheaves.

— PSALM 126:5 – 6

The wintry sky depressed Jake as he seeded the crop. The dream of a harvest supper seemed a long way off.
At home his wife was struggling to feed their baby. Her frustration all but smothered hopes for the full-grown son he would become. Then evening came, and they sat beside the fire and silently warmed their dreams together.

Ezra 1:1–6
Psalm 126
Luke 8:16–18

SEPTEMBER 25

*Let the governor and the elders of the Jews continue the
work on that house of God; they are to rebuild it on
its former site.*

— EZRA 6:7

As trees in the forest, we are constantly called
to draw strength and wisdom from our
deepest roots—from the words and example
of those whose hearts were first set alight by
your love, and who took the first steps
along your way.

Ezra 6:7–8, 12, 14–20
Psalm 122
Psalm 126

SEPTEMBER 26

• SAINTS COSMAS AND DAMIAN, MARTYRS •

*He summoned the Twelve and gave them power and
authority over all demons and to cure diseases, and he sent
them to proclaim the kingdom of God and to heal (the
sick). He said to them, "Take nothing for the journey,
neither walking stick, nor sack, nor food, nor money."*

— LUKE 9:1–3

Why can we not heal and save our brothers and
sisters as you commissioned us to do? Is it
because the hands we need for the task are so
full with the many things we are trying to take
with us on the journey?

Ezra 9:5–9
Tobit 13:2, 3–4, 6, 7–8, 6
Luke 9:1–6

Thursday

SEPTEMBER 27

Now thus says the LORD of hosts:
Consider your ways!
You have sown much, but have brought in little;
you have eaten, but have not been satisfied;
You have drunk, but have not been exhilarated;
have clothed yourselves, but not been warmed;
And he who earned wages
earned them for a bag with holes in it.

— HAGGAI 1:5 – 6

When I put my money in the bank, Lord, help me to
remember that I am dealing with a dangerously addictive
substance that, without your grace, will leave me
forever longing for more.

Haggai 1:1–8
Psalm 149
Luke 9:7–9

• SAINT WENCESLAS, MARTYR • SAINT LAWRENCE RUIZ, MARTYR, AND HIS
COMPANIONS, MARTYRS •

Once when Jesus was praying in solitude, and the disciples
were with him, he asked them, "Who do the crowds say that I am?"
They said in reply, "John the Baptist; others, Elijah; still others,
'One of the ancient prophets has arisen.'" Then he said to them, "But
who do you say that I am?"

— LUKE 9:18 – 20

The five-year-olds were coming out of school at the end of
their first day. "Which one's your mom?" David asked Jim.
"I know her. She's the lady at the checkout in the
supermarket," broke in Simon. "No, she's our Sunday school
teacher," David corrected him. Only Jim knew the full
truth. He ran up to her and gave her a big hug, because
only he knew who she really was.

Haggai 1:15–2:9
Psalm 43
Luke 9:18–22

Saturday

SEPTEMBER 29

• SAINTS MICHAEL, GABRIEL, AND RAPHAEL, ARCHANGELS •

*"Amen, amen, I say to you, you will see the sky opened
and the angels of God ascending and descending on
the Son of Man."*

— JOHN 1:51

Heaven can open up in unexpected places,
shedding gleams of eternity upon the cobbled
paths of every day. Angels can whisper
prompts to holiness in hearts that are battered
by life's storms. Please give us eyes to see
heaven's gleaming and ears to hear the
murmuring of angels.

Daniel 7:9–10, 13–14 or Revelation 12:7–12
Psalm 138
John 1:47–51

⇒ 277 ⇐

Woe to the complacent in Zion,
to the overconfident on the mount of Samaria. . . .
they shall be the first to go into exile,
and their wanton revelry shall be done away with.

— AMOS 6:1, 7

Just as I begin to feel safe and sure in your
presence, something happens to rekindle some
forgotten fear or some unhelpful distraction.
I lose my footing and fall victim to the landslide,
only to tumble, bruised and tearful, to the
foot of the mountain, and there to find myself
received into your waiting arms again.

Amos 6:1, 4–7
Psalm 146
1 Timothy 6:11–16
Luke 16:19–31

Jesus realized the intention of their hearts and took a child and placed it by his side and said to them, "Whoever receives this child in my name receives me, and whoever receives me receives the one who sent me. For the one who is least among all of you is the one who is the greatest."

— LUKE 9:47 – 48

In all the huge world I have built around myself, is there still room for the little child I once was, who was small enough to capture all the wonder of the present moment? Help me welcome her for your sake, and in welcoming her, let me welcome you.

Zechariah 8:1–8
Psalm 102
Luke 9:46–50

Tuesday

OCTOBER 2

• THE GUARDIAN ANGELS •

"Amen, I say to you, unless you turn and become like
children, you will not enter the kingdom of heaven.
Whoever humbles himself like this child is the greatest in the
kingdom of heaven."

— MATTHEW 18 : 3 – 4

Janice had spent 90 percent of the day either
going back over yesterday or planning for
tomorrow. Her little son, on the other hand, had
spent every single moment in the wonder of
today. As she kissed him good night, she asked
herself which of them had really been living.

Zechariah 8:20–23
Psalm 91
Matthew 18:1–5, 10

———————

Wednesday

OCTOBER 3

But how could we sing a song of the LORD
in a foreign land?
If I forget you, Jerusalem,
may my right hand wither.

— PSALM 137:4 – 5

Janice was often depressed and lonely in the
nursing home. She had only her memories to
nourish her spirit, but in those memories
were the pearls of experience that had made
her life precious, and nothing could wrest
them from her.

Nehemiah 2:1–8
Psalm 137
Luke 9:57–62

───────────────

⋟ 281 ⋞

Thursday

OCTOBER 4

• SAINT FRANCIS OF ASSISI, RELIGIOUS •

*He said further: "Go, eat rich foods and drink sweet drinks,
and allot portions to those who had nothing prepared; for
today is holy to our LORD. Do not be saddened this day,
for rejoicing in the LORD must be your strength!"*

— NEHEMIAH 8:10

You ask only this of those who come to your
table: that we enjoy your feast and that
we share it.

Nehemiah 8:1–12
Psalm 19
Luke 10:1–12

How long, LORD? Will you be angry forever?
Will your rage keep burning like fire? . . .
Do not hold past iniquities against us;
may your compassion come quickly,
for we have been brought very low.

— PSALM 79:5, 8

The hurt child becomes the hurting parent,
in a chain of pain that only your grace can break.
How long, O Lord, before we allow your
healing compassion to meet us in the hurting?

Baruch 1:15–22
Psalm 79
Luke 10:13–16

*At that very moment he rejoiced (in) the holy Spirit and
said, "I give you praise, Father, Lord of heaven and
earth, for although you have hidden these things from the
wise and the learned you have revealed them to
the childlike."*

— LUKE 10:21

As we build the mountains of knowledge in our
children's minds, help us to tread carefully,
lest we bury the treasure of wisdom that you
have planted in their hearts.

Baruch 4:5–12, 27–29
Psalm 69
Luke 10:17–24

*And the apostles said to the Lord, "Increase our faith." The
Lord replied, "If you have faith the size of a mustard seed,
you would say to (this) mulberry tree, 'Be uprooted and
planted in the sea,' and it would obey you."*

— LUKE 17:5 – 6

A tiny grain of faith can be enough to uproot the
weeds of fear and doubt that choke our hearts.
And a tiny mustard seed can flavor the whole pot
of soup in which our lives are lived.

Habakkuk 1:2–3; 2:2–4
Psalm 95
2 Timothy 1:6–8, 13–14
Luke 17:5–10

This is the word of the LORD that came to Jonah, son of Amittai: "Set out for the great city of Nineveh, and preach against it; their wickedness has come up before me." But Jonah made ready to flee to Tarshish away from the LORD. He went down to Joppa, found a ship going to Tarshish, paid the fare, and went aboard to journey with them to Tarshish, away from the LORD. The LORD, however, hurled a violent wind upon the sea, and in the furious tempest that arose the ship was on the point of breaking up.

— JONAH 1:1 – 4

I know when I am trying to avoid your stirrings in
my life and running away from your guiding. I know
it because the turmoil inside me rises to storm
force and my life starts to fly apart.

Jonah 1:1–2:1, 11
Psalm 2
Luke 10:25–37

• SAINT DENIS, BISHOP AND MARTYR, AND HIS COMPANIONS, MARTYRS •
SAINT JOHN LEONARDI, PRIEST •

Martha, burdened with much serving, came to him and said, "Lord, do you
not care that my sister has left me by myself to do the serving? Tell
her to help me." The Lord said to her in reply, "Martha, Martha, you are
anxious and worried about many things. There is need of only one
thing. Mary has chosen the better part and it will not be taken from her."

— LUKE 10:40 – 42

By evening, Christine felt exhausted and fragmented.
She felt as if she had been all things to all people: wife,
mother, colleague, friend, secretary, teacher, and
nurse. She lay awake in bed, too tired to sleep, and watched
the sky. One single star shone out above her. It steadied
her heart, until she could hear your voice inside her:
"For me, you are one; you are whole; you are Christine."

Jonah 3:1–10
Psalm 130
Luke 10:38–42

Wednesday
OCTOBER 10

*He was praying in a certain place, and when he had
finished, one of his disciples said to him, "Lord, teach us to
pray just as John taught his disciples."*

— LUKE 11:1

We learn to pray by being in the presence of the
One who is always in his Father's presence.

Jonah 4:1–11
Psalm 86
Luke 11:1–4

OCTOBER 11

"What father among you would hand his son a snake when he asks for a fish? Or hand him a scorpion when he asks for an egg? If you then, who are wicked, know how to give good gifts to your children, how much more will the Father in heaven give the holy Spirit to those who ask him?"

— LUKE 11:11–13

One of the best parts of Christmas is choosing those little gifts that the recipient hasn't even thought to ask for. When I choose gifts like that, I remember the surprises of your Spirit that you choose for us and place along our path, for the sheer joy of giving.

Malachi 3:13–20
Psalm 1
Luke 11:5–13

The nations fall into the pit they dig;
in the snare they hide, their own foot is caught.

— PSALM 9:16

There is a causal connection between the greed
and pride of empire and the barbarity and
squalor of war. There is a causal connection
between our every selfish gesture and the deep
discontent that reigns in and around us.

Joel 1:13–15; 2:1–2
Psalm 9
Luke 11:15–26

Saturday

OCTOBER 13

And then, on that day,
the mountains shall drip new wine,
and the hills shall flow with milk;
And the channels of Judah
shall flow with water.

— JOEL 4:18

When God breaks out inside us, something
overflows: nourishing, intoxicating, unceasingly
replenished. Then God is in flood, and there
will be an abundant harvest.

Joel 4:12–21
Psalm 97
Luke 11:27–28

So Naaman went down and plunged into the Jordan seven times at the word of the man of God. His flesh became again like the flesh of a little child, and he was clean. He returned with his whole retinue to the man of God. On his arrival he stood before him and said, "Now I know that there is no God in all the earth, except in Israel. Please accept a gift from your servant." "As the LORD lives whom I serve, I will not take it."

— 2 KINGS 5:14–16

There is nothing we can give you in gratitude for our healing, except to live out the fullness of lives made whole again, as reflections of your love.

2 Kings 5:14–17
Psalm 98
2 Timothy 2:8–13
Luke 17:11–19

Sing a new song to the LORD,
who has done marvelous deeds.

— PSALM 98:1

The world has turned through thousands of years since life began, yet still the song of every life is uniquely new and fresh, and brings joy to you, our creator.

Romans 1:1–7
Psalm 98
Luke 11:29–32

⇒ 293 ⇐

The Pharisee was amazed to see that [Jesus] did not observe the prescribed washing before the meal. The Lord said to him, "Oh you Pharisees! Although you cleanse the outside of the cup and the dish, inside you are filled with plunder and evil."

— LUKE 11:38 – 39

Aunt Agatha kept an immaculate household and insisted on orderly behavior in her home. She cringed as her small nephew came bursting in from the garden with muddy feet and sticky hands. But her protests were stifled by his exuberant hug, and the stiffness in her heart was softened by the warmth of his dirty face.

Romans 1:16–25
Psalm 19
Luke 11:37–41

My soul rests in God alone,
from whom comes my salvation.
God alone is my rock and salvation,
my secure height; I shall never fall.

— PSALM 62:2 – 3

Beneath the most turbulent waves of my life lie
the still and silent ocean depths of prayer.
And beneath the depths, I find you, my seabed,
my rock, and my place of rest.

Romans 2:1–11
Psalm 62
Luke 11:42–46

*"I am sending you like lambs among wolves. Carry no
money bag, no sack, no sandals."*

— LUKE 10:3 – 4

When I carry nothing, I am freed of the
fear of loss, and there is space in my heart and
my life through which your love can flow.

2 Timothy 4:10–17
Psalm 145
Luke 10:1–9

[Jesus] began to speak, first to his disciples, "Beware of the leaven—that is, the hypocrisy—of the Pharisees. There is nothing concealed that will not be revealed, nor secret that will not be known. Therefore whatever you have said in the darkness will be heard in the light, and what you have whispered behind closed doors will be proclaimed on the housetops."

— LUKE 12:1 – 3

One worm can make the apple bad. One bit of yeast can make the loaf rise. Our lies can multiply into a torrent of evil, but our truth can swell the ocean of redeeming love.

Romans 4:1—8
Psalm 32
Luke 12:1—7

I tell you, everyone who acknowledges me before others the Son of Man
will acknowledge before the angels of God. But whoever denies me before
others will be denied before the angels of God.

— LUKE 12:8 – 9

Max was always kind to the young prisoners of war who
had been forcibly drafted into his place of work. He risked
his own life to make their burden lighter, and he did it
quietly and without fuss. When the war ended and the
conquering armies stormed the city, there was little mercy
for the former oppressors. But those ex-prisoners
remembered Max. They spoke up for him, their humanity
acknowledging his. A life for a life.

Romans 4:13, 16—18
Psalm 105
Luke 12:8—12

OCTOBER 21

The LORD is your guardian;
the LORD is your shade
at your right hand.
By day the sun cannot harm you,
nor the moon by night.

— PSALM 121:5 – 6

In those parts of our life that seem like
empty deserts, we feel the extremes of the desert
climate: the burning pain of anger or
disappointment; the cold darkness of despair. But
you, who made both sun and moon, hold us
in the far greater orbit of your unchanging love.

Exodus 17:8–13
Psalm 121
2 Timothy 3:14–4:2
Luke 18:1–8

Then he told them a parable. "There was a rich man whose land produced a bountiful harvest. He asked himself, 'What shall I do, for I do not have space to store my harvest?' And he said, 'This is what I shall do: I shall tear down my barns and build larger ones. There I shall store all my grain and other goods.' . . . But God said to him, 'You fool, this night your life will be demanded of you and the things you have prepared, to whom will they belong?'"

— LUKE 12:16 – 19, 20

Jane worked tirelessly for charity, raising funds and stirring people into action. She committed more and more of her time and energy to this all-consuming passion. By the time she got to bed each night she was too exhausted to hear the sobbing of her little son, lying alone with his fears in the next room.

Romans 4:20–25
Luke 1:69–70, 71–72, 73–75
Luke 12:13–21

Tuesday

OCTOBER 23

• SAINT JOHN OF CAPISTRANO, PRIEST •

The law entered in so that transgression might increase but,
where sin increased, grace overflowed all the more.

— ROMANS 5:20

We try to carry your grace up the mountains
of our lives like a liter of water in a plastic bottle,
and we pass by the unnoticed and untasted
streams of your living spirit.

Romans 5:12, 15, 17–21
Psalm 40
Luke 12:35–38

Wednesday

OCTOBER 24

• SAINT ANTHONY MARY CLARET, BISHOP •

We escaped with our lives
like a bird from the fowler's snare;
the snare was broken and we escaped.

— PSALM 124:7

When I receive your gift of freedom, Lord, do I
let its power carry me on eagle's wings, or
do I tremble at the cage door like a stranded
cockatiel, unable to risk a life beyond captivity?

Romans 6:12–18
Psalm 124
Luke 12:39–48

For the wages of sin is death, but the gift of God is eternal
life in Christ Jesus our Lord.

— ROMANS 6:23

Will I choose the predictable wage of fleeting
satisfaction paid by my slave master, sin,
or will I risk the unimaginable, unpredictable,
once-and-forever gift of your grace?

Romans 6:19–23
Psalm 1
Luke 12:49–53

He also said to the crowds, "When you see (a) cloud rising in the west you say immediately that it is going to rain—and so it does. . . . You know how to interpret the appearance of the earth and the sky; why do you not know how to interpret the present time?"

— LUKE 12:54,56

The early Polynesian explorers navigated the Pacific Ocean by reading the stars, watching the clouds, and feeling the swell of the tides beneath their boats. How much more surely shall the constellations of our own circumstances, the moods and movements of our hearts be our God-given guides today on our journey of discovery toward him?

Romans 7:18–25
Psalm 119
Luke 12:54–59

And he told them this parable: "There once was a person who had a fig tree planted in his orchard, and when he came in search of fruit on it but found none, he said to the gardener, 'For three years now I have come in search of fruit on this fig tree but have found none. (So) cut it down. Why should it exhaust the soil?' He said to him in reply, 'Sir, leave it for this year also, and I shall cultivate the ground around it and fertilize it; it may bear fruit in the future. If not you can cut it down.'"

— LUKE 13:6 – 9

John's daughter was dyslexic. Already in her
early years she had been dismissed as an
underachiever, and that might have been the end
of the road for her. John thought back over the
long evenings spent at home encouraging her to
read and to express herself. And his heart
warmed with a father's love and care as he
watched her graduation ceremony.

Romans 8:1–11
Psalm 24
Luke 13:1–9

Sunday

OCTOBER 28

"Two people went up to the temple area to pray; one was a Pharisee and the other was a tax collector. The Pharisee took up his position and spoke this prayer to himself, 'O God, I thank you that I am not like the rest of humanity—greedy, dishonest, adulterous—or even like this tax collector. I fast twice a week, and I pay tithes on my whole income.'
But the tax collector stood off at a distance and would not even raise his eyes to heaven but beat his breast and prayed, 'O God, be merciful to me a sinner.'"

— LUKE 18:10 – 13

When I think of the things that I do best in life and
feel the satisfaction of doing them better than my friends
or colleagues, then I meet my inner Pharisee, who
points her finger at me with the words, "And you thought
you were a tax collector!"

Sirach 35:12–14, 16–18
Psalm 34
2 Timothy 4:6–8, 16–18
Luke 18:9–14

Monday

OCTOBER 29

Father of the fatherless, defender of widows —
this is the God whose abode is holy,
Who gives a home to the forsaken,
who leads prisoners out to prosperity.

— PSALM 68:6 – 7

We need to know the ache of loneliness
before we can receive the full depth of your
companionship. We need to know how it
feels to be trapped before we can savor the taste
of your freedom. Our pain is the passport
to a greater joy.

Romans 8:12–17
Psalm 68
Luke 13:10–17

OCTOBER 30

Again he said, "To what shall I compare the kingdom of God? It is like yeast that a woman took and mixed (in) with three measures of wheat flour until the whole batch of dough was leavened."

— LUKE 13:20 – 21

The packet of yeast stood beside the bag of flour on the kitchen table. It thought to itself, "I'm so glad I'm yeast, with my special gifts to transform flour into bread." Then the baker took it in his hands and crumbled it into tiny fragments, dissolved it in warm water, and mixed it into the flour, until it was totally broken down and lost. Give us the grace to allow the yeast in us to be crumbled, mingled, and lost in the flour of our lived lives and still to trust the promised transformation.

Romans 8:18–25
Psalm 126
Luke 13:18–21

OCTOBER 31

We know that all things work for good for those who love
God, who are called according to his purpose.

— ROMANS 8:28

The falling leaves, the rotting berries, the
crushed acorns seem to hold all our regrets and
disappointments in their autumn dying. But
they also hold our dreams and hopes and faith
within their seeding.

Romans 8:26–30
Psalm 13
Luke 13:22–30

*"These are the ones who have survived the time of great
distress; they have washed their robes and made them white
in the blood of the Lamb."*

— REVELATION 7:14

Your saints, Lord, are not those who have never
failed and fallen, but those who have had the
honesty and courage to face their fallenness and
admit their need of you and to let your love
cleanse them.

Revelation 7:2–4, 9–14
Psalm 24
1 John 3:1–3
Matthew 5:1–12

*If, then, we have died with Christ, we believe that we shall
also live with him.*

— ROMANS 6:8

What a rich comfort that, not only do we
dwell with Christ but also with all those brothers
and sisters who have preceded us in both
life and death.

Daniel 12:1–3
Psalm 27
Romans 6:3–9 or 6:3–4, 8–9
John 6:37–40 or any readings taken from Masses for the dead, nos. 1011–1016

*"For everyone who exalts himself will be humbled, but the
one who humbles himself will be exalted."*

— LUKE 14:11

Tourists wait in line to visit the palace.
Tomorrow their day will be just a memory. Once
it was the other way round, and kings lined up to
visit a stable. We are still talking about their visit
two thousand years later.

Romans 11:1–2, 11–12, 25–29
Psalm 94
Luke 14:1, 7–11

Sunday

NOVEMBER 4

The LORD is trustworthy in every word,
and faithful in every work.
The LORD supports all who are falling
and raises up all who are bowed down.

— PSALM 145:13 – 14

Jake was getting old and feeling the strain in his back.
But his garden was his pride and joy. After the storm,
he put on his boots and went out to tend his
plants. Lovingly, he bound up those that had been
flattened by the wind and supported them with canes
and twine. Those that had snapped completely he
brought into the house, putting the broken flowers in a vase
and taking new cuttings from the shattered plants. It was
his sacrament of faith, of hope, and of love.

Wisdom 11:22–12:2
Psalm 145
2 Thessalonians 1:11–2:2
Luke 19:1–10

*Oh, the depth of the riches and wisdom and knowledge of
God! How inscrutable are his judgments and how
unsearchable his ways!
"For who has known the mind of the Lord;
or who has been his counselor?"*

— ROMANS 11:33 – 34

Your wisdom rises beyond us as the stars above
the highest mountain peak. Yet still, Lord, we try
to advise you on how to arrange your world and
the details of our little lives. Still we try to
capture the vastness of your purpose within the
cramped cages of our minds.

Romans 11:29–36
Psalm 69
Luke 14:12–14

Tuesday

NOVEMBER 6

• ELECTION DAY •

*[S]o we, though many, are one body in Christ and
individually parts of one another.*

— ROMANS 12:5

We stand together, each one a link in the circle
of life, each needing our neighbors, each
holding our neighbors, and all held in God.

Romans 12:5–16
Psalm 131
Luke 14:15–24

NOVEMBER 7

"You shall love your neighbor as yourself." Love does no evil to the neighbor; hence, love is the fulfillment of the law.

— ROMANS 13:9 – 10

Love hurts. Love brings us up against our
most painful choices. Love strips away our masks
and exposes our deepest truth. And precisely
because of that, love heals.

Romans 13:8–10
Psalm 112
Luke 14:25–33

"*What man among you having a hundred sheep and losing one of them would not leave the ninety-nine in the desert and go after the lost one until he finds it? . . . I tell you, in just the same way there will be more joy in heaven over one sinner who repents than over ninety-nine righteous people who have no need of repentance.*"

— LUKE 15:4, 7

Ted had all he needed, but still he spent most of his time in his old rocking chair. It was polished with age and wear now, but he would never forget that, years ago, he had found it, mildewed, splintered and abandoned, at the dump. It had taken him years to restore it, and now it meant everything to him. He had invested his heart in it and made it live again.

Romans 14:7–12
Psalm 27
Luke 15:1–10

*He made a whip out of cords and drove them all out of the temple area,
with the sheep and oxen, and spilled the coins of the money-changers and
overturned their tables, and to those who sold doves he said, "Take these
out of here, and stop making my Father's house a marketplace."*

— JOHN 2:15 – 16

In the marketplace of life one commodity stands apart
from all the rest—your love and your grace have no
price tag. And at the end of the day, when the market stalls
are dismantled, that one commodity will still be there,
because however many people have drawn on it, there is
always more.

Ezekiel 47:1–2, 8–9, 12
Psalm 84
1 Corinthians 3:9–11, 16–17
John 2:13–22 or any readings taken from the Common of the
Dedication of a Church, numbers 701–706

*The person who is trustworthy in very small matters is also
trustworthy in great ones; and the person who is dishonest
in very small matters is also dishonest in great ones.*

— LUKE 16:10

If I can trust you with the burdens of my heart,
I do not need to wonder whether I can trust you
with the contents of my purse.

Romans 16:3–9, 16, 22–27
Psalm 145
Luke 16:9–15

*"[H]e is not God of the dead, but of the living, for to him
all are alive."*

— LUKE 20:38

In a garden there is no death, but only the falling
of seed to the waiting earth. Lord, not of our
dead darkness, but of the seeds you have planted
there, let our gardens live!

2 Maccabees 7:1–2, 9–14
Psalm 17
2 Thessalonians 2:16–3:5
Luke 20:27–38 or 20:27, 34–38

Monday

NOVEMBER 12

• SAINT JOSAPHAT, BISHOP AND MARTYR •

Even before a word is on my tongue,
LORD, you know it all.
— PSALM 139:4

When I express my needs and hopes and fears in
the words of my prayer, I know that you hear
my call. But when I lay before you the nakedness
of what I cannot express, then you enfold me
in the deepest knowledge of your heart.

Wisdom 1:1–7
Psalm 139
Luke 17:1–6

Tuesday

NOVEMBER 13

• SAINT FRANCES XAVIER CABRINI, VIRGIN •

The LORD's face is against evildoers
to wipe out their memory from the earth.
When the just cry out, the LORD hears
and rescues them from all distress.

— PSALM 34:17–18

It had been a grim day. As she climbed into bed,
Jean nearly sank under the depressing weight of mistakes,
misjudgments, and harsh, unnecessary words. But that
moment of kindness from a passing stranger had made her
feel more kindly to her fellow human beings, and that
new shoot on the camellia bush had made her feel more
kindly to herself. She switched off the light and let
the destructive things fade out of remembrance and turned
her eyes instead to those moments of light.

Wisdom 2:23–3:9
Psalm 34
Luke 17:7–10

⇒ 323 ⇐

As he was entering a village, ten lepers met (him). They stood at a distance from him and raised their voice, saying, "Jesus, Master! Have pity on us!" And when he saw them, he said, "Go show yourselves to the priests." As they were going they were cleansed. And one of them, realizing he had been healed, returned, glorifying God in a loud voice; and he fell at the feet of Jesus and thanked him. He was a Samaritan. Jesus said in reply, "Ten were cleansed, were they not? Where are the other nine? Has none but this foreigner returned to give thanks to God?"

— LUKE 17:12 – 18

The visiting preacher had made a profound impression on the congregation. Philip hung back. It was the first time he had been inside a church for years, and the sermon had knocked him sideways. Slowly, he slipped back into the empty church, knelt down, and let his joy flow out in tears.

Wisdom 6:1–11
Psalm 82
Luke 17:11–19

Asked by the Pharisees when the kingdom of God would come, he said in reply, "The coming of the kingdom of God cannot be observed, and no one will announce, 'Look, here it is,' or, 'There it is.' For behold, the kingdom of God is among you."

— LUKE 17:20 – 21

Hour by hour your kingdom comes, silently, imperceptibly, powerfully as springtime, with all the fragile determination of the butterfly emerging from the caterpillar. We are called, not to watch anxiously for its coming, but joyfully to recognize its ever-present reality.

Wisdom 7:22–8:1
Psalm 119
Luke 17:20–25

Remember the wife of Lot. Whoever seeks to preserve his life
will lose it, but whoever loses it will save it.

— LUKE 17:32 – 33

I tried to protect myself behind a mask of
cynicism but became corroded by its salt sting.
I tried to hide my hurting in a pool of
vinegary sarcasm, but I drowned in its acid
depths. Only when I let go my anxious
grip on my own fears and frenzies did I discover
the joy of flying free.

Wisdom 13:1–9
Psalm 19
Luke 17:26–37

Saturday

NOVEMBER 17

• SAINT ELIZABETH OF HUNGARY, RELIGIOUS •

The cloud overshadowed their camp
and out of what had before been water, dry land was seen emerging:
Out of the Red Sea an unimpeded road,
and a grassy plain out of the mighty flood.
Over this crossed the whole nation sheltered by your hand,
after they beheld stupendous wonders.

— WISDOM 19:7–8

The clouds of mess and muddle seem to make our way
impassable. But like the mists of morning they give way to a
breathtaking sunrise, and in the distance we begin to
glimpse the promise of dry land beyond our wildest storms.

Wisdom 18:14–16; 19:6–9
Psalm 105
Luke 18:1–8

⋛ 327 ⋚

NOVEMBER 18

For lo, the day is coming, blazing like an oven,
when all the proud and all evildoers will be stubble,
And the day that is coming will set them on fire,
leaving them neither root nor branch,
says the LORD of hosts.
But for you who fear my name, there will arise
the sun of justice with its healing rays.

— MALACHI 3:19 – 20

Out of the harvest of our lives, the stubble of
our failure. Out of the stubble of failure, the smoke of our
shame. Out of the smoke of shame, the ashes of hope.
And out of the ashes, the nutrients for the new life, waiting
for the healing rays of the sun and a new beginning.

Malachi 3:19–20
Psalm 98
2 Thessalonians 3:7–12
Luke 21:5–19

———————

*But many in Israel were determined and resolved in their
hearts not to eat anything unclean;
they preferred to die rather than to be defiled with unclean
food or to profane the holy covenant;
and they did die. Terrible affliction was upon Israel.*

—1 MACCABEES 1:62 – 64

There was a good degree and a bright future
offered to those who were willing to spy on their
friends and denounce them to the totalitarian
authorities. Yet at the start of the next term, only
half of them returned to college. The rest had
gone: some to freedom, some to death.

1 Maccabees 1:10–15, 41–43, 54–57, 62–64
Psalm 119
Luke 18:35–43

*[Zacchaeus] was seeking to see who Jesus was; but he could not see him
because of the crowd, for he was short in stature. So he ran ahead and
climbed a sycamore tree in order to see Jesus, who was about to pass that
way. When he reached the place, Jesus looked up and said to him,
"Zacchaeus, come down quickly, for today I must stay at your house."*

— LUKE 19:3 – 5

My only thought was to get a little closer to you, to
get a better view. Yet that unspoken desire was all
you needed to bring you to the very spot where I was so
precariously perched. "I'm looking for companions," you
said, "not onlookers. Are you coming down?"

2 Maccabees 6:18–31
Psalm 3
Luke 19:1–10

"I tell you, to everyone who has, more will be given, but from the one who has not, even what he has will be taken away."

— LUKE 19:26

Moira was barely strong enough to get out of her hospital
bed. But with what energy she could muster she went
round to her fellow patients with words of encouragement.
One by one they responded, with a smile, the clasp
of a hand, a shared word, a tear, a glance of understanding.
As she climbed back into bed, everyone in the ward had
been enriched by her love, and a quiet new energy
was flowing with a power that defied their weakness.

2 Maccabees 7:1, 20–31
Psalm 17
Luke 19:11–28

NOVEMBER 22

• THANKSGIVING DAY • SAINT CECILIA, VIRGIN AND MARTYR •

As he [Jesus] drew near, he saw the city and wept over it,
saying, "If this day you only knew what makes for
peace—but now it is hidden from your eyes . . . because
you did not recognize the time of your visitation."

— LUKE 19:41 – 42, 44

The phone call came a few moments too
late. The car wouldn't start. There was a holdup
on the highway. By the time he rushed into the
intensive care unit his brother had just died.
The word of forgiveness would never be spoken.
Never again. His heart cracked . . . if only!

1 Maccabees 2:15–29
Psalm 50
Luke 19:41–44

• SAINT CLEMENT I, POPE AND MARTYR • SAINT COLUMBANUS, ABBOT •
BLESSED MIGUEL AGUSTÌN PRO, PRIEST AND MARTYR •

Then Jesus entered the temple area and proceeded to drive
out those who were selling things, saying to them, "It is
written, 'My house shall be a house of prayer, but you
have made it a den of thieves.' "

— LUKE 19:45 – 46

There were whispered mutterings about the
stranger at the back of the church. She had a
"past." She wasn't entirely nice to know.
What was she doing in church anyway, they
wondered? She sensed the hostility and
slipped quietly off into the shadows. Something
of great value had been stolen from her—and
that on consecrated ground!

1 Maccabees 4:36–37, 52–59
1 Chronicles 29:10–12
Luke 19:45–48

———————————

*When the king heard this news [of his defeat], he was
struck with fear and very much shaken. Sick with grief
because his designs had failed, he took to his bed.*

—1 MACCABEES 6:8

How it amazes us, Lord, when our
plans don't coincide with yours, and how it
shakes us when life fails to conform to
our requirements. How it must have surprised
our ancestors, too, when they discovered
that the earth revolves around the sun and not
the sun around the earth.

1 Maccabees 6:1–13
Psalm 9
Luke 20:27–40

The people stood by and watched; the rulers, meanwhile, sneered at him and said, "He saved others, let him save himself if he is the chosen one, the Messiah of God."

— LUKE 23:35

It was hard for Mark to imagine, as he watched his father dying in agonizing pain and disfigurement, that his dad had lived out his life as a surgeon whose touch had saved so many others. Then the end came, and as the stricken doctor gave back his life breath to God, his face relaxed into a peace beyond understanding. It was in that moment that Mark understood the difference between truly healing and merely curing.

2 Samuel 5:1–3
Psalm 122
Colossians 1:12–20
Luke 23:35–43

[Jesus] noticed a poor widow putting in two small coins. He said, "I tell you truly, this poor widow put in more than all the rest; for those others have all made offerings from their surplus wealth, but she, from her poverty, has offered her whole livelihood."

— LUKE 21:2–4

Joan sat down thankfully for half an hour with a book and a cup of coffee, an oasis of peace and space for herself before the children came home from school. As always, the day had gone by in a whirlwind of jobs, one crowding out the other, and the evening would be the same. But this was her time and her space, the only bit she had. Then the phone rang. Maureen was in tears at the other end of the line. She needed a friend. Joan set her book aside and gave her space to one who needed it even more than she did.

Daniel 1:1–6, 8–20
Daniel 3:52–56
Luke 21:1–4

Tuesday

NOVEMBER 27

"See that you not be deceived, for many will come in my name, saying, 'I am he,' and 'The time has come.' Do not follow them!"

— LUKE 21:8

Some of the imposters live in my own mind, Lord. They tell me I ought to do this or that, be someone different, convert the world to my own way of thinking, and they say it all in your name. Sometimes they clamor so loudly that I can barely hear the still small voice of your real self, deep in my heart.

Daniel 2:31–45
Daniel 3:57–61
Luke 21:5–11

337

"[T]hey will seize and persecute you . . . and they will
have you led before kings and governors because of my
name. It will lead to your giving testimony. Remember, you
are not to prepare your defense beforehand, for I myself
shall give you a wisdom in speaking that all your
adversaries will be powerless to resist or refute."

— LUKE 21:12 – 15

In our human speaking we are so often merely
ourselves. But when we allow our human
being to speak through our gestures and our
silences, we are making space for the wisdom
of your Word to shine through.

Daniel 3:62–67
Daniel 5:1–6, 13–14, 16–17, 23–28
Luke 21:12–19

*[H]is kingdom shall not be destroyed, and his dominion
shall be without end.
He is a deliverer and savior,
working signs and wonders in heaven and on earth.*

— DANIEL 6:27 – 28

National sovereignty: defending our corner
against the others? Personal sovereignty:
surrendering our corner to your kingdom!

Daniel 3:68–74
Daniel 6:12–28
Luke 21:20–28

Friday

NOVEMBER 30

• SAINT ANDREW, APOSTLE •

*As he was walking by the Sea of Galilee, he saw two
brothers, Simon who is called Peter, and his brother
Andrew, casting a net into the sea; they were fishermen. He
said to them, "Come after me, and I will make you fishers of
men." At once they left their nets and followed him.*

— MATTHEW 4:18 – 20

The personal skills with which we earn our
living become, under your leadership,
the specific gifts by which you call us to bless
creation with your loving.

Romans 10:9–18
Psalm 19
Matthew 4:18–22

———————

"Be vigilant at all times and pray that you have the strength to escape the tribulations that are imminent and to stand before the Son of Man."

— LUKE 21:36

I guard myself against drought not by filling up my spare bottles with water, but by remaining close to the spring.

Daniel 3:82, 83, 84, 85, 86, 87
Daniel 7:15–27
Luke 21:34–36

He shall judge between the nations,
and impose terms on many peoples.
They shall beat their swords into plowshares
and their spears into pruning hooks;
One nation shall not raise the sword against another,
nor shall they train for war again.

— ISAIAH 2:4

Liz smiled wryly as she recalled her student days. She had been radical, even violent, in her demonstrations against the injustice of the system. There had been a time for wielding the sword of protest, she reflected as she opened up the homeless shelter for the night, but now was the season for binding wounds, not for inflicting them.

Isaiah 2:1–5
Psalm 122
Romans 13:11–14
Matthew 24:37–44

Monday

DECEMBER 3

• SAINT FRANCIS XAVIER, PRIEST •

*I say to you, many will come from the east and the west,
and will recline with Abraham, Isaac, and Jacob at the
banquet in the kingdom of heaven.*

— MATTHEW 8:11

The dinner guests were carefully screened to
avoid social embarrassment. The conversation
was suitably polite and the atmosphere a
little chilled. Down the road at the hostel the
men shivered as they wrapped thankful hands
round bowls of hot soup; friendly banter
warmed up the raw night air. It was a feast,
because love sat among them.

Isaiah 4:2–6
Psalm 122
Matthew 8:5–11

⋛ 343 ⋚

"Blessed are the eyes that see what you see. For I say to
you, many prophets and kings desired to see what you see,
but did not see it, and to hear what you hear,
but did not hear it."

— LUKE 10:23 – 24

When we catch a glimpse of you in a baby's first
grasp or an old man's memories, in the first
crocus or the last autumn rose, we see what no
book can contain or human wisdom can reveal.

Isaiah 11:1–10
Psalm 72
Luke 10:21–24

———————————

"Behold our God, to whom we looked to save us!
This is the LORD for whom we looked."
— ISAIAH 25:9

A tremor of joy always ran through Jennie's heart
as she assisted at a birth. Every newborn
child seemed to be a carrier of the unspoken
hopes of all humanity. In a little speck of life
was a hope for a better future. How much
more powerful then the hope that is born in you,
the bringer of eternal life?

Isaiah 25:6–10
Psalm 23
Matthew 15:29–37

"Not everyone who says to me, 'Lord, Lord,' will enter the kingdom of heaven, but only the one who does the will of my Father in heaven."

— MATTHEW 7:21

My prayer ended, so I thought, with a heartfelt promise to you to mend that strained relationship. The real prayer began when I saw her coming toward me in the street and faced my desire to avoid the meeting.

Isaiah 26:1–6
Psalm 118
Matthew 7:21, 24–27

The LORD is my light and my salvation;
whom do I fear?
The LORD is my life's refuge;
of whom am I afraid?
— PSALM 27:1

When I stand in the full light of the noonday
sun, I do not worry about whether my
flashlight battery might fail. Then, Lord,
knowing you to be the ground of my
being, may I let go of the many lesser matters
that pull me down into anxiety?

Isaiah 29:17–24
Psalm 27
Matthew 9:27–31

Saturday

DECEMBER 8

• THE IMMACULATE CONCEPTION OF THE BLESSED VIRGIN MARY •

*"The holy Spirit will come upon you, and the power
of the Most High will overshadow you. Therefore the child
to be born will be called holy, the Son of God."*

— LUKE 1:35 – 36

When your Spirit brings our hopes and dreams
to life, then they will surely grow into fruits
of your kingdom.

Genesis 3:9–15, 20
Psalm 98
Ephesians 1:3–6, 11–12
Luke 1:26–38

Then the wolf shall be a guest of the lamb,
and the leopard shall lie down with the kid;
The calf and the young lion shall browse together,
with a little child to guide them. . . .
There shall be no harm or ruin on all my holy mountain;
for the earth shall be filled with knowledge of the LORD,
as water covers the sea.

— ISAIAH 11:6, 9

For two minutes the whole nation was silent, honoring the memory of their assassinated leader. At the graveside of this man who had lived and died for peace, his former enemies stood alongside his supporters, while his grandchild spoke her simple words of love.

Isaiah 11:1–10
Psalm 72
Romans 15:4–9
Matthew 3:1–12

DECEMBER 10

The desert and the parched land will exult;
the steppe will rejoice and bloom.

— ISAIAH 35:1

There is an inner desert where my branches
fade and fail in the heat of the sun and my leaves
wither. It is there that my roots reach down
in their great need for the untapped well of the
groundwater, which alone can bring to life
the hidden seeds in my heart.

Isaiah 35:1–10
Psalm 85
Luke 5:17–26

A voice cries out:
In the desert prepare the way of the LORD!
Make straight in the wasteland a highway for our God!

— ISAIAH 40:3

When the Berlin Wall came down, most of it was
crushed to produce what turned out to be the
finest quality road-making material. The
roadblocks of oppression can be turned into the
steppingstones of peace.

Isaiah 40:1–11
Psalm 96
Matthew 18:12–14

⇒ 351 ⇐

Wednesday

DECEMBER 12

• SAINT JANE FRANCES DE CHANTAL, RELIGIOUS • OUR LADY OF
GUADALUPE •

*For at the moment the sound of your greeting reached my
ears, the infant in my womb leaped for joy.*

— LUKE 1:44

Your greetings wait to surprise us around every
corner of our living and in every moment of our
days. And every time we recognize them,
your life, growing in our hearts, leaps for joy
and comes a little closer to its birth.

Zechariah 2:14–17 or Revelation 11:19; 12:1–6, 10
Psalm 45
Luke 1:26–38 or Luke 1:39–47 or any readings from the
Common of the Blessed Virgin Mary, nos. 707–712

———————————

For I am the LORD, your God,
who grasps your right hand;
It is I who say to you, "Fear not,
I will help you."

— ISAIAH 41:13

Everyone could hear the hysterical sobbing amid the crowd of Christmas shoppers, but no one could quite see where it was coming from. Then the child's mother made her way through the mass of people, gently but with firm determination. She reached out to take hold of her toddler's hand. At once the sobbing stopped, and all was well.

Isaiah 41:13–20
Psalm 145
Matthew 11:11–15

*"To what shall I compare this generation? It is like children
who sit in marketplaces and call to one another, 'We
played the flute for you, but you did not dance, we sang a
dirge but you did not mourn.' "*

— MATTHEW 11:16 – 17

I notice that my most desolate moods descend
when the world won't dance to my tune or cry
over my little troubles, and that I feel most
at peace when I am so absorbed in the music, or
the sorrow, of another, that I forget to think
about my own.

Isaiah 48:17–19
Psalm 1
Matthew 11:16–19

[R]evive us, and we will call on your name.
— PSALM 80:19

We do not call upon your name in order
that you might give us life. Rather, it is your
gift of life, welling up inside us, that makes
us able to call out to you, the source
of everything we are.

Sirach 48:1–4, 9–11
Psalm 80
Matthew 17:10–13

Sunday

DECEMBER 16

• THIRD SUNDAY OF ADVENT •

When John heard in prison of the works of the Messiah, he sent his disciples to him with this question, "Are you the one who is to come, or should we look for another?" Jesus said to them in reply, "Go and tell John what you hear and see: the blind regain their sight, the lame walk, lepers are cleansed, the deaf hear, the dead are raised, and the poor have the good news proclaimed to them."

— MATTHEW 11:2 – 5

When we see the life-giving power of your
healing in our lives, we do not need to
ask who you are.

Isaiah 35:1–6, 10
Psalm 146
James 5:7–10
Matthew 11:2–11

That the mountains may yield their bounty for the people,
and the hills great abundance.

— PSALM 72:3

The most fertile soil in the area had had its
ancient origins in a volcanic eruption that had
brought devastation in its wake. So too,
Lord, our worst upheavals are often the source
of our richest growth.

Genesis 49:2, 8–10
Psalm 72
Matthew 1:1–17

[T]he angel of the Lord appeared to him in a dream and said, "Joseph, son of David, do not be afraid to take Mary your wife into your home. For it is through the holy Spirit that this child has been conceived in her."

— MATTHEW 1:20

It frightens us too, Lord, and it can frighten those around us, when your seed starts to grow in our hearts. Give us the courage to embrace your deepest truths and take them home.

Jeremiah 23:5–8
Psalm 72
Matthew 1:18–24

≥ 358 ≤

*"He will . . . turn the hearts of fathers toward children
and the disobedient to the understanding of the righteous, to
prepare a people fit for the Lord."*

— LUKE 1:17

Turning back to you will always challenge us to
turn back to each other. There cannot be the
one without the other.

Judges 13:2–7, 24–25
Psalm 71
Luke 1:5–25

*Mary said, "Behold, I am the handmaid of the Lord. May
it be done to me according to your word."*

— LUKE 1:38

She gave you the blank check of her life. You
cashed it in. You took everything she had,
and more, and left her grieving at the foot of the
cross. And then you returned her capital
with so much interest that all the world could
live on it from that day forward.

Isaiah 7:10–14
Psalm 24
Luke 1:26–38

*"Blessed are you who believed that what was spoken to you
by the Lord would be fulfilled."*

— LUKE 1:45

Ben paused for a moment's rest after planting his
spring bulbs. There was only a bare patch of
earth to mark all his efforts. But he knew what
would be there in the springtime. That
knowledge—beyond sight and reason—
transformed his labor and transfigured the bare
earth into a place of faith and blessing.

Song of Songs 2:8–14 or Zephaniah 3:14–18
Psalm 33
Luke 1:39–45

*Once he [Samuel] was weaned, she [Hannah] brought him
up with her . . . [to] the temple of the LORD. . . . "I
prayed for this child, and the LORD granted my request.
Now I, in turn, give him to the LORD; as long as he lives,
he shall be dedicated to the LORD." She left him there.*

—1 SAMUEL 1:24, 27–28

The test of the purity of my prayer is this:
When you give me what I ask of you,
can I immediately let it go again? And can
I do so with joy?

1 Samuel 1:24–28
1 Samuel 2:1, 4–8
Luke 1:46–56

[T]he virgin shall be with child, and bear a son, and shall name him Immanuel.

— ISAIAH 7:14 – 15

Nothing would ever be quite the same again when the baby was born. An entirely new and unpredictable stage of our lives had begun, which was to bring difficulties, decisions, heartaches, and great joy. This new presence in our lives would, from this day forward, be with us in every moment, waking and sleeping, and would change our lives irreversibly. You, too, come silently into our hearts when the time is right, changing us at our roots. Once you have become God-with-us, we can never again be without you.

Isaiah 7:10–14
Psalm 24
Romans 1:1–7
Matthew 1:18–25

DECEMBER 24

"[T]he tender mercy of our God
by which the daybreak from on high will visit us
to shine on those who sit in darkness and death's shadow,
to guide our feet into the path of peace."

— LUKE 1:77–79

To be in your presence is to become gradually
bathed in your light, as surely as to stand in the
dawn is to see the darkness melt into the
daylight. We can do nothing to bring your light
to our hearts. We can only wait and trust in
your promise of its coming.

2 Samuel 7:1–5, 8–12, 14, 16
Psalm 89
Luke 1:67–79

"For today in the city of David a savior has been born for you who is Messiah and Lord. And this will be a sign for you: you will find an infant wrapped in swaddling clothes and lying in a manger."

— LUKE 2:11–12

We wrap our gifts in glittering paper and adorn them with ribbons, hoping to make what is really very ordinary look like something special. Your gift to us, your incarnate Word, comes barely wrapped at all. You give us that which is utterly special, but you wrap it in ordinariness, so that we won't be afraid to receive it.

VIGIL:
Isaiah 62:1–5
Psalm 89
Acts 13:16–17, 22–25
Matthew 1:1–25 or 1:18–25

MIDNIGHT:
Isaiah 9:1–6
Psalm 96
Titus 2:11–14
Luke 2:1–14

DAWN:
Isaiah 62:11–12
Psalm 97
Titus 3:4–7
Luke 2:15–20

DAY:
Isaiah 52:7–10
Psalm 98
Hebrews 1:1–6
John 1:1–18 or 1:1–5, 9–14

Wednesday

DECEMBER 26

• SAINT STEPHEN, FIRST MARTYR •

*But he [Stephen], filled with the holy Spirit, looked up intently to heaven
and saw the glory of God and Jesus standing at the right hand of God,
and he said, "Behold, I see the heavens opened and the Son of Man
standing at the right hand of God." But they cried out in a loud voice,
covered their ears, and rushed upon him together. They threw him out of
the city, and began to stone him.*

— ACTS 7:55 – 58

As I walked through the barracks of Auschwitz-Birkenau,
I felt that I was walking on holy ground. In that place there
had been those who had joined their walk to death
with yours. They had walked through the jaws of hell and
yet seen the gates of heaven.

Acts 6:8–10; 7:54–59
Psalm 31
Matthew 10:17–22

⋛ 367 ⋜

What was from the beginning,
what we have heard,
what we have seen with our eyes,
what we looked upon
and touched with our hands
concerns the Word of life.

—1 JOHN 1:1

He reached out to me in my distress, and my
eyes met his. I saw the human friend, so
completely familiar to me, but I saw, too, the
mystery of the unknowable God, interpreted for
me by his love.

1 John 1:1–4
Psalm 97
John 20:2–8

[T]he angel of the Lord appeared to Joseph in a dream and said, "Rise, take the child and his mother, flee to Egypt, and stay there until I tell you. Herod is going to search for the child to destroy him."

— MATTHEW 2:13 – 14

"Where's the baby Jesus?" little Paul asked his parents, his voice full of disbelief as he gazed at the crib in the church on Christmas morning. The day passed, dinner was over, the new games had been played, and evening came. The family watched the television news. "There's the baby Jesus!" exclaimed Paul with conviction, pointing to the pictures of a refugee family fleeing with their baby, the sound of gunfire at their heels.

1 John 1:5–2:2
Psalm 124
Matthew 2:13–18

[Simeon] took him into his arms and blessed God, saying:
"Now, Master, you may let your servant go in peace,
according to your word,
for my eyes have seen your salvation."

— LUKE 2:28 – 30

We recognize you when we take you to ourselves
and touch your Reality, and that happens
when we take each other to ourselves and bless
the Christ who is at once both hidden and
revealed in our brothers and sisters. Such
moments are blessed. They open the doors to
the peace that passes understanding.

1 John 2:3–11
Psalm 96
Luke 2:22–35

Let the word of Christ dwell in you richly.

— COLOSSIANS 3:16

Tangled up in all the conflicting demands of our
lives, we forget that the richest treasure of all
asks nothing more of us than a little space in our
hearts where he may be at home.

Sirach 3:2–6, 12–14
Psalm 128
Colossians 3:12–21 or Colossians 3:12–17
Matthew 2:13–15, 19–23

Let the heavens be glad and the earth rejoice;
let the sea and what fills it resound;
let the plains be joyful and all that is in them.
Then let all the trees of the forest rejoice
before the LORD who comes,
who comes to govern the earth.

— PSALM 96:11–13

In the last hours of the dying year our hearts and our homes break out in celebration to welcome the new. The winter trees are gestating the coming springtime, and you, Lord, are coming to claim us as your own.

1 John 2:18–21
Psalm 96
John 1:1–18